crochet

crochet

Designs by
Stephanie J. Milne

MURDOCH BOOKS

contents

techniques

projects

Introduction

The word 'crochet' is derived from the Middle French *croc* or *croche*, meaning hook, and describes a process of making fabric from thread, yarn or cord using a special type of hook. Crochet is one of the most recent textile processes. Although other woven, knitted and knotted textiles survive from early times, there are no examples of crochet as we know it today that can be dated earlier than about 1800. Other early forms of needlework produced similar results, but used quite different techniques. Crochet may have developed from tambour embroidery (in which a chain stitch was worked through fabric using a small hook) when someone realised that the chains thus formed would hold together without the background fabric.

Whatever its origins, the earliest known examples of true crochet began appearing in Europe in the early 1800s. The craft rapidly caught on, especially as a quick and easy substitute for old-style needle lace and bobbin lace designs that were much slower to produce. By the early 1840s, a huge variety of instructions for crochet was being published in England, and crochet became a thriving cottage industry in many countries. However, it was at first perceived by many as a cheap substitute for lace made by older and more expensive methods, rather than admired as a craft in its own right. This impression later lessened, in part due to the influence of Queen Victoria, who promoted the craft by buying Irish crocheted laces and even learned to crochet herself.

Even today, despite a recent resurgence in popularity, crochet is sometimes regarded as the poor relation of knitting. This is an unfortunate perception, given that crochet is easy to learn, easy and comparatively quick to do, and lends itself much better than knitting to freeform designs. Making curves and three-dimensional forms (some of them elaborate and highly sculptural), improvising shapes and working in the round are all much easier to do in crochet than in knitting.

After enormous popularity in the Victorian and Edwardian periods, crochet began to decline in the inter-war years, then to regain popularity from the 1940s onwards. In the last few years it has undergone a revival, partly due to the great variety of interesting yarns now available.

crocheted flowers Round and three-dimensional shapes such as these are easy to crochet.

Types of crochet

Some types of crochet require only a hook and yarn; in others (such as broomstick and hairpin crochet), the yarn is wound around another tool, then the crochet stitches are formed with the hook.

Broomstick crochet (also known as broomstick lace) This technique combines the use of a crochet hook and another long, slender item (traditionally a broomstick, but now more usually a thick knitting needle or a piece of craft dowel). The foundation of the piece is a chain, into which are worked loops that are then transferred to the knitting needle or dowel. Several loops are then crocheted together and slipped off the dowel, creating a soft but stable fabric.

Cro-hook This special double-ended crochet hook is used to make double-sided crochet. The hook has two ends, allowing two colours of yarn to be handled at once and freely interchanged.

Filet crochet A type of crochet consisting of filled and open meshes constructed from chain and treble crochet stitches. The way in which the filled and open meshes are arranged creates an infinity of possible patterns. It is usual for open mesh to form the background and for the pattern to be created in filled mesh. Filet crochet instructions are generally given as charts rather than words.

Hairpin crochet (also known as hairpin lace) In this technique, lace is made using a crochet hook and a small U-shaped metal loom (formerly a hairpin was used, hence the name). Yarn is wrapped around the prongs of the loom, and one crochets into the middle of the loops to create a strip of lace. The strips thus formed can then be joined to create a lightweight fabric.

Irish crochet An intricate and beautiful type of lace in which motifs are crocheted separately, laid out and tacked onto a temporary background fabric, then joined using crochet mesh. Sometimes, parts of the motifs are reinforced with cord to give extra definition. In mid-19th century Ireland, in the wake of the devastating potato famine, the craft was encouraged as a cottage industry to provide income for families that might otherwise have been destitute. Families often had their own carefully guarded designs; a unique pattern was worth more money.

Tunisian crochet (also known as Afghan crochet) In this technique, stitches are formed in two parts. Working from right to left, a loop is picked up in each stitch across the row without being worked off the hook. At the end of the row, and working from left to right, the yarn is drawn through two loops at a time, thus completing each stitch. This technique creates a dense fabric with a definite right and wrong side.

Yarns and threads

Any yarn that is suitable for knitting can be used for crochet. Yarns may be natural, synthetic or a mixture of both. Natural yarns are derived either from animals (including wool, mohair, alpaca and angora), or plants (including hemp, linen, soy silk, corn silk and bamboo). Synthetic yarns include rayon, nylon, acrylic and polyester, and are often combined with natural fibres to enhance their performance or texture. Each fibre has its own inherent characteristics, which the manufacturer may modify in various ways during processing; for example, yarns can be treated and spun to make them fluffier, denser, flatter, shinier or more twisted.

When choosing a yarn, there are several factors to consider. Beginners will find it easier to work with a smooth yarn than a highly textured one. A smooth yarn is also the best choice for an intricate pattern, as a highly textured or novelty yarn will mask the beautiful details of the piece. If you wish to use one of the many interesting textured or 'busy' yarns that are available, choose a simple stitch pattern so that the yarn itself is the focus of the finished article.

Consider also the use to which the finished item will be put. For an easy-care garment, for example, choose a machine-wash yarn; this will ensure that the garment does not felt and shrink when it is washed. Cotton also wears and washes well. Items made of delicate yarns should be gently hand-washed or, in some cases, dry-cleaned only. The ball band — the piece of paper that comes wrapped around the ball of yarn when you buy it — will tell you how the garment should be treated, as well as the composition of the yarn, the weight of the ball and the length of yarn it contains, among other things.

The terms used to describe yarns vary from country to country. The following conversion chart may be useful.

yarns and threads The term 'yarn' usually refers to thicker fibres and 'thread' to thinner ones, although the terms are sometimes interchanged. Clockwise from the top are various yarns: fine mohair, DK-weight mercerized cotton, aran-weight Tencel, aran-weight cotton, cashmere–merino mix, and alpaca. In the centre are two spools of mercerized cotton thread.

Some terms used to describe yarn refer to its content (such as wool, cashmere, cotton) and others (such as bouclé, tweed, aran) to its texture, finish and/or thickness.

Crochet uses about 30 per cent more yarn than knitting.

International yarn equivalents Note that figures given are approximate and will vary between manufacturers and individual crocheters. Tension is expressed as the number of stitches per 10 cm (4 in) over double crochet/dc (US single crochet/sc).

Weight	Australia/NZ	USA	UK and Canada	Tension	Hook
Super-fine	2 or 3-ply	Sock, fingering, baby	Lace weight, sock	21–32 sts	2.25–3.5 mm
Fine	4 or 5-ply	Sport, baby	Sport	16–20 sts	3.5–4.5 mm
Light	8-ply	Double knitting (DK), light worsted	Double knitting (DK)	12–17 sts	4.5–5.5 mm
Medium	10-ply	Worsted weight, afghan, aran	Aran	11–14 sts	5.5–6.5 mm
Bulky	12-ply	Chunky, craft, rug	Chunky	8–11 sts	6.5–9 mm
Super bulky	14-ply plus	Bulky, roving	Super chunky	5–9 sts	9 mm or larger

Hooks

Crochet hooks come in various sizes and materials. The thinnest hooks, used with very fine yarns, are made of steel. Larger hooks are made from aluminium, plastic or bamboo. No one material is superior to another; they are simply different, and you should use whichever material suits you better. People with arthritis, for example, may prefer plastic hooks to the colder and slightly heavier metal ones.

Crochet hook sizes are expressed differently from country to country; see the table at left. The patterns in this book give hook sizes in metric (millimetres) followed by the equivalent US and pre-metrification UK/Canadian sizes. Sometimes there will be more than one equivalent for a metric size. The hook size is often printed or stamped onto the flattened part in the middle of the hook's shaft. If not, the shaft of the hook can be inserted into the holes in a knitting-needle gauge to determine the size. Hooks vary slightly in size between manufacturers; always be guided by your tension square rather than the nominal size of the hook.

For any yarn, the size of crochet hook needed will be larger than that of the knitting needle recommended on the ball band; this is because a crochet stitch consists of three threads of fabric, unlike a knitted stitch, which comprises only two.

Other equipment

As well as hooks of various sizes, the following will be useful:

Blunt-ended wool needle Used for darning in ends of yarn and for sewing seams. Choose a needle with an eye large enough to take your chosen yarn.

Dressmaker's pins Glass-headed pins are preferable to plastic-headed ones, as they will not melt if you accidentally press them with an iron.

Knitting needle gauge Useful for measuring crochet hooks that do not have the size printed or stamped on them.

Ruler To obtain an accurate measurement when measuring a tension square, use a ruler (which is inflexible) rather than a tape measure, which may stretch or warp.

Safety pins To hold together two pieces of crochet while joining them.

Scissors A small pair with sharp points is best.

Tape measure Choose a pliable one with both metric and imperial measures.

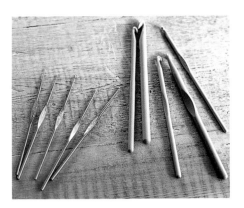

types of hook Fine metal hooks are used with fine cotton threads; aluminium, bamboo or plastic hooks are used with thicker yarns.

Metric	UK Yarn	UK Cotton	US Yarn	US Cotton
0.6 mm		7, 7½, 8		14
0.75 mm		6½		13
1 mm		6, 5½		11, 12
1.25 mm		4½, 5		9, 10
1.5 mm		3½, 4		7, 8
1.75 mm		2½, 3		6
2 mm	14	1½, 2		4, 5
2.25 mm	13			
2.5 mm	12	0, 1	0, 1	B, 1, 2, 3
2.75 mm				
3 mm	11	3/0, 2/0	2	C, 0
3.25 mm	10			
3.5 mm	9		3, 4	D, E
3.75 mm	–			
4 mm	8		5	F
4.5 mm	7		6	G
5 mm	6		7	
5.5 mm	5		8	H
6 mm	4		9	I
6.5 mm	3			
7 mm	2		10	J, K
8 mm	0		11, 12	L
9 mm	00		13, 15	M, N
10 mm	000		15	N, P
15 mm				P, Q

Holding the hook and yarn

There is no one 'right' way to hold the hook or yarn; you should do so in any way that is comfortable, lets you obtain an even tension and allows the yarn to flow freely. Aim to hold the hook gently and comfortably, about a third of the way down the shaft, rather than gripping it tightly. Shown below are two common holds.

Holding the yarn

Holding the yarn is also a matter of personal choice and comfort. The yarn needs to flow freely and not be stretched, which may change the gauge to which it works. The way in which you hold the yarn should also be comfortable enough to be sustained through a long crocheting session; if your hands cramp up frequently, try various holds until you find one that suits you better.

Two possible methods of holding the yarn are shown below left. In the first, the yarn is run over the ring finger, under the second finger and over the index finger. In the second, the yarn is run under the middle two fingers and around the little finger.

knife hold One method is to hold the hook as you would a knife.

pen hold Alternatively, hold the hook as you would a pen.

one method of holding the yarn The yarn is laced between the fingers.

alternative method The ball end of the yarn is wound around the little finger.

Hints

When making loops around the hook, do so along the main part of the shaft, rather than close to the head of the hook, where the hook is narrower. If you do the latter, your stitches will be too small.

Unless otherwise instructed, the yarn is always put over the hook before being caught and pulled through. If the yarn is taken under the hook and then caught, the stitch produced will look different from that in the pattern.

The basic stitches

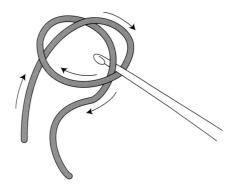

Crochet can be worked either flat, as shown on the following pages, or in rounds (see page 22). When crochet is worked flat, it is turned at the end of each row; the fabric thus produced is the same or very similar on both front and back. When working in the round, however, the work is not turned; the same side of the work always faces you, and the appearance of back and front will be quite different. Usually, the flatter side is considered the 'right' side, but if you prefer the other side, by all means use that as the front of the work.

Making a slip knot

Make a loop in a length of yarn. Bring the yarn up from back to front through the loop and pull to tighten. You have now made a slipknot. Place the loop on the crochet hook. You can now begin making a crochet chain. Remember that the slip knot is not included when counting how many chain stitches you have made.

Chain

The chain is the basis of all crochet, whether it is worked flat or in the round. The chains worked at the start of a piece of crochet are known as foundation chain.

1 First, make a slip knot (see left) and put it onto the crochet hook.

2 Insert the hook under then over the yarn and draw the yarn through the loop of the slip knot. You have created one chain stitch. Repeat as required.

Note When counting foundation chains, the initial slip stitch is not counted.

step two Insert hook under then over yarn and draw the yarn through the loop on the hook.

the completed chain stitch Repeat Step 2 until you have the required length of chain.

back and front The front of the chain forms a smooth series of V shapes; the back looks bumpy.

Turning chain

Chains are also used at the beginning of a row or round, to lift the hook up to the same height as the stitches that are to be worked in the next row or round. These are known as turning chain. The various crochet stitches are each of a different height, so the number of turning chain worked depends on the height of the stitch in use. You will generally need to work one chain for double crochet, two chain for half-treble crochet, three chain for treble crochet, and so on. See also Hint at right.

Chain mesh or lace

Chains are also used to make lacy patterns, or to separate one block or group of stitches from another, creating a mesh effect. To produce a series of arches, several chains are worked, then a double crochet or slip stitch is made into the row below; these steps are repeated to the end of the row.

Slip stitch

The slip stitch is essentially a chain that is worked into another stitch or another part of the fabric. It is used to join a round of crochet, and also to move the hook from one position to another, as when making motifs; it forms a barely visible link between one area and the next, particularly useful when creating lacy motifs.

Hint

When working trebles or longer stitches using yarn rather than cotton, you may find that you need one less turning chain than the pattern specifies. Work a small sample first, or experiment with your tension swatch. Should working the specified number of turning chain result in a curved edge or a small hole at the beginning of a row, try working one less turning chain to see if the effect is better.

slip stitch Insert the hook into the fabric, then catch the yarn with the hook.

slip stitch, continued Draw the yarn through both the fabric and the loop on the hook.

slip stitch fabric When worked in rows or rounds, slip stitch creates a very dense fabric.

Double crochet

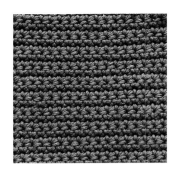

Double crochet (dc) — known in the United States as single crochet (sc) — produces a fabric that is firm, dense and stable, yet also flexible. When worked in rows, as shown right, a distinct horizontal pattern is created.

When working in double crochet, the number of foundation chain should equal the number of stitches required, plus one for the turning chain. Hold the chain with the smooth side facing you.

1 Insert the hook from front to back through the second chain from the hook, picking up two strands of chain. Wrap the yarn over the hook (yoh).

2 Draw the yarn through the chain to the front; there will be two loops on the hook. Wrap yarn over hook again.

3 Draw the yarn through both loops on the hook. You have now completed one double crochet stitch. One loop will remain on the hook.

4 Repeat Steps 1 to 3 to the end of the row, working one double crochet into each chain. At the end of the row, turn and work 1 turning chain; this counts as one stitch, so the first double crochet of the second row is worked into the second stitch of the previous row.

5 When working back along the row, insert the hook under both loops of each stitch in the previous row.

step one Insert the hook into the second chain from the hook, then wrap the yarn over the hook.

step two Draw the yarn through the chain (two loops on hook). Wrap the yarn over the hook again.

start of second row Turn, work 1 turning chain, insert hook in second stitch of previous row.

last stitch of a row This is worked into the turning chain at the start of the previous row.

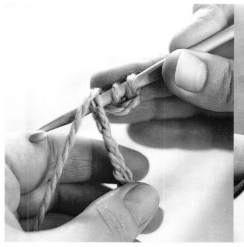

Half treble crochet

Half treble crochet (htr) — known in the United States as half double crochet (hdc) — produces a fabric that is flexible, yet less dense than double crochet. When working in half treble crochet, the number of foundation chain should equal the number of stitches required, plus two for the turning chain. Hold the chain with the smooth side facing you.

1 Wrap the yarn over the hook and insert the hook into the third chain from the hook, picking up two strands of chain. Wrap the yarn over the hook.

2 Draw the yarn through the chain to the front; there will be three loops on the hook. Wrap the yarn over the hook again.

3 Draw the yarn through all three loops on the hook. You have now completed one half treble crochet. One loop will remain on the hook.

4 Repeat Steps 1 to 3 to the end of the row, working one half treble crochet into each chain. At the end of the row, turn and work two turning chain; these count as one stitch, so the first half treble crochet of the second row is worked into the second stitch of the previous row.

5 When working back along the row, insert the hook under both loops of each stitch in the previous row.

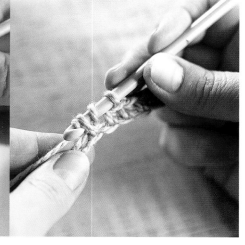

step one Wrap the yarn over the hook and insert it into the third chain from the hook.

step two Draw yarn through chain (three loops on hook), then wrap the yarn over the hook again.

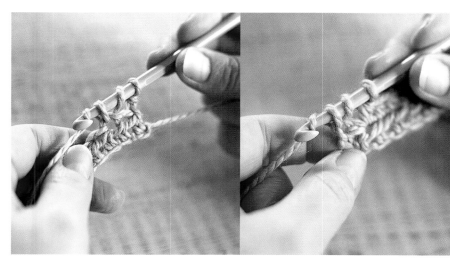

start of second row Work 2 turning chain, yarn over hook, insert hook into second stitch.

last stitch of a row This is worked into the top of the turning chain at the start of the previous row.

Treble crochet

Treble crochet (tr) —known in the United States as double crochet (dc) — produces a flexible, slightly open fabric. When working in treble crochet, the number of foundation chain should equal the number of stitches required, plus three for the turning chain. Hold the chain with the smooth side facing you.

1 Wrap the yarn over the hook and insert the hook into the fourth chain from the hook, picking up two strands of chain. Wrap the yarn over the hook.

2 Draw the yarn through the chain to the front; there will be three loops on the hook. Wrap the yarn over the hook again.

3 Draw the yarn through two loops on the hook. Wrap the yarn over the hook again and then draw it through two more loops. You have now completed one treble crochet stitch. One loop will remain on the hook.

4 Repeat Steps 1 to 3 to the end of the row, working one treble crochet into each chain. At the end of the row, turn and work three turning chain; these count as one stitch, so the first treble crochet of the second row is worked into the second stitch of the previous row.

5 When working back along the row, insert the hook under both loops of each stitch in the previous row.

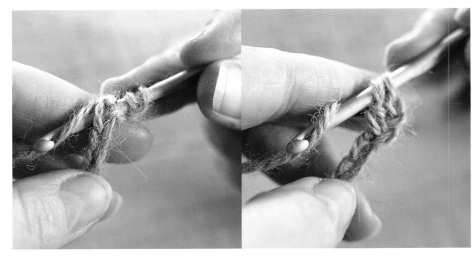

step one Wrap yarn over hook, insert it in third chain from hook, and wrap yarn over hook again.

step two Draw yarn though chain, yarn over hook, draw yarn through two loops on hook, yarn over hook.

end of first row At the end of the row, work three turning chain.

end of subsequent rows Work the last stitch of a row into the top of the turning chain.

Double treble

Double treble crochet (dtr) — known in the United States as treble crochet (tr) — is usually used in combination with other stitches rather than to form a fabric on its own.

When working in double treble crochet, the number of foundation chain should equal the number of stitches required, plus four for the turning chain.

1 Wrap the yarn over the hook twice and insert the hook into the fifth chain from the hook, picking up two strands of chain. Wrap the yarn over the hook.

2 Draw the yarn through the chain to the front; there will be four loops on the hook. Wrap the yarn over the hook again.

3 Draw the yarn through two loops on the hook, *wrap yarn over hook and draw it through two more loops.* Repeat from * to * once. You have now completed one double treble stitch. One loop remains on the hook.

4 Repeat Steps 1 to 3 to the end of the row, working one double treble crochet into each chain. At the end of the row, turn and work four turning chain; these count as one stitch, so the first double treble of the second row is worked into the second stitch of the previous row. Work the last stitch of each row into the the top of the turning chain of the previous row.

step one Yarn over hook twice, insert hook into fifth chain from hook, yarn over hook.

step two Draw the yarn through the chain to the front. Wrap yarn over hook.

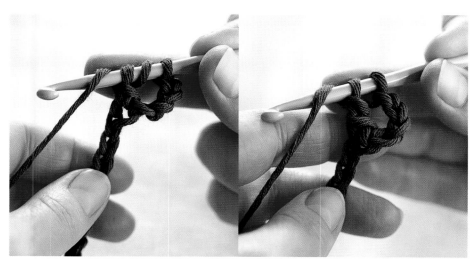

step three Yoh and draw through two loops on hook. Repeat once.

step three, continued Yoh and draw through two loops on hook.

Triple treble

Triple treble crochet (trtr) is known in the United States as double treble crochet (dtr). When working in triple treble crochet, the number of foundation chain should equal the number of stitches required, plus five for the turning chain.

1 Wrap the yarn over the hook three times, then insert the hook into the sixth chain from the hook. Draw the yarn through the chain to the front.

2 *Yarn over hook, draw through two loops on hook*, repeat from * to * until only one loop remains on hook.

3 At the beginning of each row, turn, then work five turning chain. At the end of each row, work the last stitch into the top of the turning chain at the beginning of the previous row.

Quadruple treble

Quadruple treble crochet (qdtr) is known in the United States as triple treble crochet (trtr). When working in quadruple treble crochet, the number of foundation chain should equal the number of stitches required, plus six for the turning chain.

1 Wrap the yarn over the hook four times, then insert the hook into the seventh chain from the hook. Draw the yarn through the chain to the front of the work.

2 *Yarn over hook, draw through two loops on hook*, repeat from * to * until only one loop remains on the hook.

3 At the beginning of each row, turn, then work six turning chain. At the end of each row, work the last stitch into the top of the turning chain at the beginning of the previous row.

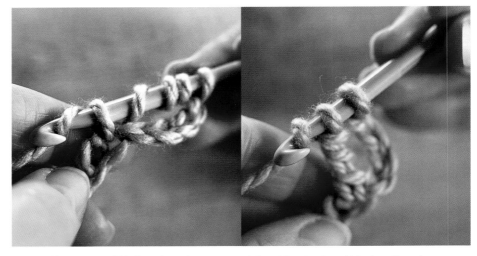

triple treble, step one Yoh three times, insert hook into sixth chain, draw yarn through.

triple treble, step two (Yoh, draw through two loops on hook) until only one loop remains.

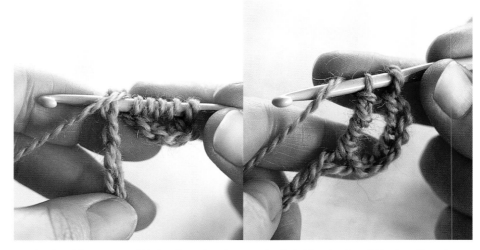

quadruple treble, step one Yoh four times, insert hook into seventh chain, draw yarn through.

quadruple treble, step two (Yoh, draw through two loops on hook) until only one loop remains.

Working groups of stitches

Working a number of stitches together produces a group (also known as a cluster). Groups can be utliized with any of the longer stitches (half treble crochet and up). They can be worked all in one type of stitch, or in a combination.

Each stitch of the group is worked until two loops remain on the hook (rather than the usual one loop). The last step of the last stitch of each group is to draw the yarn through all the loops on the hook, thus gathering the tops of all the stitches together.

Groups can be worked into a chain loop or chain space (as shown in blue yarn in the photographs at left), or into a single stitch. Alternatively, each successive stitch of the group can be worked into a separate stitch of the previous row (as shown in pink yarn). Groups are usually separated from each other with a number of chain, as shown.

1 Using the required stitch type, work a stitch until two loops remain on the hook. Repeat until you have worked the required number of stitches for that group.

At the end of this step, there should be one more loop on the hook than there are stitches in the group (for example, if working a group of four stitches as at left, you will end up with five loops on the hook).

2 Wrap the yarn over the hook and draw the yarn through all the loops on the hook. You have now completed one group.

3 Work the required number of chains to separate the group from the next.

4 Repeat Steps 1 to 3 as required.

working into a chain loop Here, each group consists of four treble crochet stitches.

last step of last stitch yoh and draw the yarn through all the loops on the hook.

working into successive stitches Work one stitch into each stitch of the previous row.

Increases

To make an internal increase along a row, work to where the increase is required, then work two or more stitches into the same stitch. To shape garment edges neatly, this method is used one stitch in from the edge at the beginning or end of a row. At the beginning of a row, work the first stitch, then work the increase in the next stitch. At the end of the row, work until two stitches remain, work the increase in the second-last stitch, then work the last stitch.

To make an external increase at the start of a row, work the required number of chains at the end of the previous row (remember to include the turning chain), then turn and work along the row as usual. At the end of a row, leave the last few stitches unworked. Remove the hook, join a length of yarn to the last stitch of the row, and work the required number of extra chains (remember to include the turning chain). Fasten off. Insert the hook back into the row, complete the row, then work the extra stitches along the chain.

Shaping techniques

A piece of crochet is shaped by increasing or decreasing. Increases are made by working two or more stitches into the same stitch of the previous row. Decreases are made by skipping stitches, or by working two or more stitches together. These shapings are described as 'internal' when made along a row, and 'external' when made at the beginning or end of a row. Each method produces a different effect.

internal increase along a row Work two or more stitches into the same stitch.

internal increase at edge of crochet Work the increase one stitch in from the edge.

external increase at start of row Work extra chain at end of previous row, turn, then work along row.

external increase at row end, step one Join in yarn and work required number of extra chains.

external increase at row end, step two Reinsert hook into row and work to end of chain.

Decreases

To decrease, skip one or more stitches when working across the previous row (which creates a small hole in the fabric), or work two or more stitches together. To do this, work to where the decrease is required, then work a partial stitch by working it until two loops remain on the hook. Work another partial stitch until a total of three loops remain on the hook. Wrap the yarn over the hook and draw it through all three loops on the hook. You have now decreased one stitch. To decrease two stitches at once, work three partial stitches (four loops will remain on the hook), then wrap the yarn over the hook and draw it through all four loops.

To work an external decrease at the start of a row, simply slip stitch across the number of stitches to be decreased. Work the turning chain, then continue across the row. For an external decrease at the end of a row, stop several stitches before the end of the row, then turn, work the turning chain and continue back across the row.

internal decrease along a row, method one Skip one or more stitches in the previous row.

internal decrease along a row, method two Work two or more stitches together.

external decrease at start of row Slip stitch across the required number of stitches.

external decrease at start of row, step two Work the turning chain, then continue across the row.

external decrease at end of row Stop several stitches before end of previous row, then turn.

Making and working into a ring

To make a ring, work the specified number of chain, then insert the hook into the first chain that you made and join with a slip stitch. Wrap the yarn over the hook and draw it through both the chain and the loop on the hook. You have now created a ring of chains. This becomes the centre of your crochet and is what you will work into to create the first round.

To commence the first round, make the appropriate number of turning chain. Insert the hook from front to back into the ring (not into the chain) and work the number of stitches specified in the pattern. At the end of the round, join the round by working a slip stitch into the top of the starting chain that you made at the beginning of the round.

At the end of the last row of the shape or motif, join the round with a slip stitch. Cut the yarn, leaving a tail, then draw the tail of yarn through the loop left on the hook. Pull the yarn firmly to fasten off.

Working in rounds

Crochet can easily be worked in the round to create many different shapes and motifs, both simple and elaborate. All pieces worked in the round begin with a short length of chain joined to form a ring. Successive rounds are formed from combinations of stitches and chain spaces or chain loops. The piece is worked in rounds rather than back-and-forth rows, and is never turned; the right side always faces you.

joining chain to form a ring Make a slip stitch into the first chain that you made.

working first round Work all the stitches of the first round into the centre of the ring.

end of first round Join round with a slip stitch into top of first stitch (or into the turning chain).

second round Chain loops form the foundation for the third and final round.

finished motif A simple but effective openwork flower in crisp aran-weight cotton.

Measuring tension (gauge)

Tension, or gauge, refers to the number of stitches and rows to 2.5 cm (1 in) over the crocheted fabric. Every crochet pattern will specify a gauge; always pay attention to this, as the gauge determines the size of the finished item. Every person crochets at a different tension; some people crochet loosely and others tightly. Tension may not be crucial in, say, a scarf or cushion, but it is crucial in a garment that is meant to fit precisely. It is vital to check your tension before beginning a garment. In your eagerness to get started on a project, it is tempting to skip this step, but crocheting a tension swatch may prevent the disappointment, and the waste of time and money, of a garment that does not fit.

Crocheting a tension square

The first step in every crochet project should be a tension square. Use the specified hook size and the yarn that you intend to use, whether it is the yarn recommended in the pattern or a replacement. Make a crochet chain about 15 cm (6 in) long, then work in the specified stitch until the piece is at least 15 cm (6 in) long. If the pattern is constructed from motifs, you will need to make one whole motif as instructed, then measure its diameter.

Fasten off the yarn and, if appropriate, block (see page 27) or lightly press the tension square. Insert a pin a few stitches in (do not measure from the sides, as the side edge is always slightly distorted). Avoid stretching the tension square. Measure precisely 10 cm (4 in) from the pin and place another pin at that point as a marker. Do the same vertically, placing the first pin a few rows in from the edge. Count how many stitches and rows there are between the pins; this is your tension.

If the counts are correct, go ahead and start crocheting the item. If you have more stitches than the specified tension, you are working too tightly, and your garment will be too short and too narrow. Make another tension square with a slightly larger hook, and measure again. If you have fewer stitches than specified, you are working too loosely, and your garment will be too long and too wide. Make another tension square with a slightly smaller hook, and measure again. If necessary, repeat this process more than once, until the tension is correct.

Save your tension square and use it to test how well the yarn washes and whether it can be pressed. Pin the ball band to the square, and note on the ball band if you changed the hook size to obtain the correct tension. You now have a reference for the yarn used, and for how the crocheted fabric looks and feels.

tension squares These two tension squares were crocheted by the same person, in the same 8-ply (DK) yarn, but with different-sized crochet hooks. The purple square was made using a 4.5 mm crochet hook and the blue one with a 5 mm hook. The size difference is clear even over such a small sample; over a large item or a garment, the consequences of using the incorrect tension can be ruinous.

measuring a tension square Using pins, and an inflexible ruler rather than a tape measure, mark two points precisely 10 cm (4 in) apart and count the number of stitches between the pins.

Reading diagrams

The written pattern for the motif shown
below reads as follows:

Make 5ch, join with ss to form a ring.

Round 1: 1ch, 8dc into ring, ss into ch at
beg of rnd.

Round 2: 3ch, (ss into next dc, 3ch), rep to
end, ss into 1st ch sp at beg of rnd.

Round 3: 2ch (counts as 1htr), (2tr, 1htr)
into same ch sp as ss, *(1htr, 2tr, 1htr) into
next ch sp*, rep from * to * to end, ss into
base of 2ch at beg of rnd.

Floral motif This motif can be made by
following either the instructions above or the
diagram below.

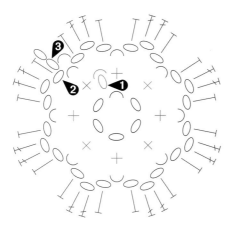

diagram of motif See opposite for a key to
the symbols used.

Working from a pattern

Crochet patterns can be either written in words or represented by symbols.
A beginner may feel safer using a written pattern. However, as you become more
adept at crochet, or when tackling large or complicated motifs, working from
a diagram may be preferable. A diagram is a visual representation of the motif
or pattern, with the symbols used replicating the stitches; as such, the diagram
will show how the motif or pattern should look in a way that words cannot.

The pattern will tell you which yarn and hook size to use, the tension required and
the size of the finished item. For a garment with more than one size, instructions
for the smallest size are given first and those for larger sizes in parentheses.

Before you begin crocheting, it is vital to work a tension square (see page 23).
You should also read through the pattern and make sure you understand all the
abbreviations used. If the pattern uses an unfamiliar stitch, practise the stitch on a
small test swatch first; it is less time consuming and frustrating to have to pull back
and redo a small piece than a large one. If using a multi-size pattern, read right
through the pattern and highlight the figures that relate to the size you are making.

Differences in terminology

Different regions use different terms for crochet; confusingly, sometimes the same
term is used for a different stitch. The following chart may help. When choosing a
pattern, first determine where it was published (this will be stated on the pattern)
and then adjust the instructions if needed. Any differences in terminology will be of
little concern if you are working from a diagram rather than a written pattern.

Australia/New Zealand/UK	United States
slip stitch	slip stitch
double crochet (dc)	single crochet (sc)
half treble (htr)	half double crochet (hdc)
treble (tr)	double crochet (dc)
double treble crochet (dtr)	treble crochet (tr)
triple treble crochet (trtr)	double treble crochet (dtr)
quadruple treble (qdtr)	treble treble (trtr) or long treble (ltr)
tension	gauge

Symbols

◯ chain

⌒ slip stitch

+ double crochet

T half treble

† treble

‡ double treble

⧣ triple treble

quadruple treble

⋀ tr2tog

⋀ tr3tog

⋁ inc 1tr

⋀ 2 half-treble group

⋀ 3 half-treble group

⋀ 4 half-treble group

⋀ 3 treble group

⋀ 3 double-treble group

⋀ 3 triple-treble group

⋀ 3 quadruple-treble group

● bead

beaded chain

beaded double crochet

 bouclé loop stitch

 solomon's knot

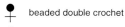 number of row/round showing direction in which you work from one row or round to the next

Abbreviations

Abbreviations are used extensively in crochet patterns to save space. Not all publications will use the same abbreviation for the same term, so read through the pattern to familiarize yourself with what each abbreviation means. Be aware that terminology differs between regions; for example, what is known as dc (double crochet) in Australia, New Zealand and the United Kingdom is called sc (single crochet) in the United States. This book uses the Australian, New Zealand and United Kingdom terminology. See opposite for some common US equivalents.

3tr group three-treble group (three incomplete treble stitches worked into one stitch before the yarn is drawn through all remaining loops on hook)

4tr group four-treble group (four incomplete treble stitches worked into one stitch before the yarn is drawn through all remaining loops on hook)

alt alternate

b/ch beaded chain

b/dc beaded double crochet

beg begin/beginning

bet between

blk block

ch chain

ch loop chain loop

ch sp chain space

cl cluster

cm centimetre(s)

col(s) colour(s)

cont continue

dc double crochet (US single crochet/sc)

dc2tog decrease 1 dc over 2 sts

dc3tog decrease 1 dc over 3 sts

dec decrease/decreasing

DK double knitting

dtr double treble

dtr group double treble group

g gram(s)

gr group

htr half treble

htr group half treble group

in inch(es)

inc increase/increasing

include include/including

lp(s) loop(s)

MC Main Colour

mm millimetre

pc picot

patt pattern

prev previous

qdtr quadruple treble

qdtr group quadruple treble group

rem remain(s)/remaining

rep repeat(s)/repeated

rnd round

RS right side(s) of work

sp(s) spaces(s)

ss slip stitch

st(s) stitch(es)

tog together

tr treble

tr group treble group

tr2tog decrease 1 tr over 2 sts

tr3tog decrease 1 tr over 3 sts

trtr triple treble

WS wrong side(s) of work

yoh yarn over hook

Finishing techniques

Crocheted pieces may be joined with sewn or crocheted seams. Each has its advantages and disadvantages, so choose the most appropriate seam for the item you are making. The pattern will generally tell you which type of seam is preferred. Sewn seams are less visible than crocheted seams, but they stretch more; they are generally best avoided in any crocheted piece that has a tendency to drop.

Oversewn seam

This method produces a very flat seam. Place the two pieces to be joined on a flat surface, with right sides up and edges aligned. Insert a large, blunt-ended needle through corresponding stitches in both pieces. The seam can be sewn through both loops of the stitch, or the back loop only.

Backstitch seam

This method produces a strong but non-elastic seam. Hold the two pieces to be joined with right sides facing. Using a large blunt-ended needle, secure the yarn by passing it around the end of the seam twice. On the next sttich, pass the needle around the back of the work and through the second stitch to the front. Pass the needle one stitch to the right, then through the fabric from the front to the back. Bring it out two stitches along and repeat for the length of the seam. (Note that stitches on the back of the fabric travel forwards and those on the front of the fabric travel backwards.)

Woven seam

Lay the pieces flat, right sides up and edges aligned. Start at the bottom and work in a ladder fashion (first from left to right, then right to left), passing the yarn through the loops of corresponding stitches. Pull the yarn tight every 2.5 cm (1 in) or so.

oversewn seam, step one Sew through loops of corresponding stitches on each piece.

oversewn seam, step two The finished seam is flat but slightly visible.

backstitch seam A backstitch seam is very sturdy, but less flexible than a crocheted seam.

woven seam When stitched in the same colour as the garment, a woven seam is almost invisible.

Crocheted seams

A crocheted seam is more visible than a sewn one, but will have a similar degree of elasticity to the rest of the item.

Crocheted seams can be worked with the right sides or the wrong sides of the pieces together, depending on the effect you wish to create. If worked with the wrong sides together, the finished seam will be visible on the right side of the item. A visible seam can be a feature on, for example, a cushion or rug (especially if worked in a contrasting colour), but may be undesirable on the outside of a garment. If in doubt, try out both methods to see which you prefer.

Double crochet seam

Hold the pieces together, having the edges even. Join in the yarn. Inserting the hook through both loops of both corresponding stitches on each side, work in double crochet for the length of the seam. If joining rows of motifs, as for a rug, join all the motifs in one direction first, then work the seam in the other direction.

Slip stitch seam

For a slightly less raised seam (not pictured), join the two pieces with slip stitch rather than double crochet.

double crochet seam, step one Work double crochet through both loops of each stitch.

double crochet seam Double crochet produces a strong, visible, raised seam.

Blocking and pressing

Blocking and pressing are methods of shaping a finished piece of crochet. They are not always necessary; check the pattern instructions, and also the yarn's ball band. Blocking and pressing are often required for crocheted lace or motifs, as they improve stitch definition and give a better shape. The extra effort required to block and press a piece is small, and will give your work a professional-looking finish.

Blocking should be done before sewing seams. To block, lay a clean, colourfast towel or sheet on a padded surface such as carpet. Lay the item to be blocked on top of this and pin it out to size, easing and gently stretching where necessary and making sure the sides and ends are completely straight.

For natural fibres such as wool or cotton, set the iron on a steam setting and hold the iron about 2.5 cm (1 in) above the farbric and allow the steam to penetrate for several seconds. Work in sections, without allowing the iron to touch the crochet. Allow to dry before removing the pins.

Pieces made from synthetic yarns should not be pressed; they will go limp, or in some cases melt. Instead, pin as described above, then spray lightly with cold water and leave to dry completely before removing the pins.

When the pins are removed, a blocked piece should be flat, the correct size, and have clearly defined stitches.

Hints

It is important, when working an edging, to space the stitches evenly so that the edge of the crocheted piece remains flat. When working an edging on a solid fabric, such as one made entirely of double crochet or treble crochet, simply work one edging stitch into each stitch along the top and bottom edges of the fabric. When working along the side edges of such fabric, or on a lacy or openwork fabric, you may need to experiment with the spacing of the edging stitches; working too few stitches will draw in the edge of the fabric, and too many stitches will produce a wavy edge.

At the end of the final row or round of any piece of crochet, cut the yarn, leaving a tail of 10–15 cm (4–6 in) — or longer if you are intending to use the tail for seaming — then draw the tail of yarn through the loop left on the hook. Pull the yarn firmly to fasten off.

Edgings

Adding an edging to your work can make all the difference to the finished item. There are many different types of edgings. As well as being decorative, edgings also act as a binding on a crocheted fabric (such as along the edge of a rug), stabilize the edge of a lacy or open fabric, or reinforce the neck, hem or armhole edge of a garment. Some edgings are worked separately, then sewn onto a woven fabric. All of the following are worked directly into the edge of a crocheted fabric, with the right side of the fabric facing you.

Double crochet edging

This is the simplest type of edging, in which one or more rows or rounds of double crochet are worked along the edge of a finished piece of crochet. When edging, for example, a rug, you might choose to work several rounds of double crochet to give a wider edging. Space the stitches evenly along the edge. When working around corners, make 3 dc into the same stitch.

Scallop edging

Also known as a shell edging, this edging should be worked over a multiple of 6 stitches. With right side of work facing, join in the yarn. *Miss 2 sts, 5tr in next st, miss 2 sts, 1ss in next st*, repeat from * to * end. Fasten off.

double crochet edging A simple edging that can be worked in one or more rounds.

scallop edging *5tr into 3rd st from hook, 1ss into 3rd st from hook*, rep from * to * to end.

crab stitch edging Crab stitch is worked as for double crochet, but backwards, from left to right.

Crab stitch edging

Crab stitch is simply a double crochet stitch worked backwards, from left to right. It is a strong, fairly rigid edging that lacks the chain-edge look of other crochet stitches, instead forming little bumps along the edge of the fabric.

With the right side of the work facing you, and keeping the yarn to the left, insert the hook into the next stitch and wrap the yarn over the hook. Draw the loop through the stitch so that there are two loops on the hook. Wrap the yarn over the hook again and draw it through both loops on the hook. One crab stitch has now been formed. Continue in this manner from left to right along the entire edge.

Picot edging

This delicate edging features small protruding loops of yarn. It can be worked directly into the edge of the fabric, or into a previous row of double crochet.

With right side of work facing, join in yarn. *1dc into next st, 3ch, 1dc into same st as previous dc, 1dc into next st*, repeat from * to * to end. Fasten off. (The distance between the picots can be altered by working more dc between them.)

Wavy edging

With right side of work facing, join in the yarn. *1dc, 1htr, 1tr, 1dtr, 1tr, 1htr*, rep from * to * until 1 st remains, 1dc. Fasten off.

Crocheted cords

Crocheted cords can be used as straps for bags, ties to secure garments, or as braids to be attached to a crocheted or sewn item. All crocheted cords will stretch; if you wish to prevent this, sew a piece of woven ribbon to the back of the crocheted cord.

The most basic crocheted cord is simply a length of crocheted chain. Other types are:

Single slip stitch cord Make a foundation chain of the required length, then work a row of slip stitches along one side of the chain.

Double slip stitch cord Make a foundation chain of the required length, then work a row of slip stitches along the first side of the chain. Work 1 turning ch, then another row of slip stitches along the second side.

Double crochet cord Make a foundation chain of the required length, then work a row of double crochet along the first side of the chain. Work 1 turning chain, then another row of double crochet along the second side.

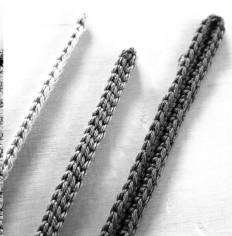

picot edging *1dc into next st, 3ch, 1dc into same st as prev dc, 1dc into next st*, rep to end.

wavy edging Stitches of differing height are worked along the edge, creating a wavy effect.

cords From left: single slip stitch cord; double slip stitch cord; double crochet cord.

Vest

Soft, silky yarn drapes nicely over the body in this pretty starburst design for a feminine singlet top. Select a yarn with a sheen in a subtle colour to make a fashion statement that will never go out of style.

Materials
150 g (5½ oz) Debbie Bliss Pure Silk

Tools
3 mm (US 2/UK 11) crochet hook

Sizes
To fit sizes S (80 cm/31½ inch chest),
    M (90 cm/35½ inch chest), L (100 cm/
    39½ inch chest)

Tension
2 rows of pattern = 14 cm wide x 7 cm high
    (5½ in wide x 2¾ in high)

Abbreviations
ch: chain
dc: double crochet
dtr: double treble
qdtr: quadruple treble
tr: treble
trtr: triple treble

BACK Sizes S (M, L)

Make 96 (112, 128)ch, turn.

Row 1 Miss 1ch, 1dc into each ch to end, turn.

Row 2 Make 3ch, *miss 1dc, 1dtr into next dc, 1ch, miss 1dc, 1trtr into next dc, 1ch, miss 1dc, 1qdtr into next dc, 1ch, miss 1dc, 1qdtr into next dc, 1ch, miss 1dc, 1trtr into next dc, 1ch, miss 1dc, 1dtr into next dc, 1ch, miss 1dc, 1tr into next dc, 1ch, miss 1dc, 1tr into next dc, 1ch*, rep from * to * to end, turn.

Row 3 Make 6ch. Working into each of the first 4 ch spaces, make a 4qdtr group; *7ch, 1dc into next ch space, 7ch; working into each of the next 7ch spaces, make a 7qdtr group*, rep from * to * another 4 (5, 6) times, 7ch, 1dc into next ch space, 7ch; working into each of the last 4ch spaces, make a 4qdtr group, turn.

Row 4 Make 6ch, 1qdtr into top of 1st qdtr group, (1ch, 1qdtr into top of same qdtr group) 4 times, *1qdtr into top of next qdtr group, 1ch, 1 qdtr into top of same qdtr group) 8 times*. Repeat from * to * another 4 (5, 6) times. 1qdtr into top of last qdtr group, (1ch, 1qdtr into top of same qdtr group) 4 times, turn.

Row 5 Make 3ch, miss 1 qdtr, *1dtr into next ch space, 1ch, 1trtr into next ch space, 1ch, 1qdtr into next ch space, 1ch, miss the ch space between the two qdtr groups, 1qdtr into next ch space, 1ch, 1trtr into next ch space, 1ch, 1dtr into next ch space, 1ch, 1tr into next ch space*, rep from * to * to end.

Repeat Rows 3–5 another 4 (5, 6) times, or until work is length desired.

Row 18 (21, 24): Shape armhole 1ss into each st until you reach the ch space between the first qdtr of the previous row, 1dc into next ch space, *7ch, 1qdtr into each of next 7ch spaces (making a 7qdtr group), 7ch, 1dc into next ch space*, rep from * to * another 4 (5, 6) times, turn.

Row 19 (22, 25) Make 6ch, 1qdtr into top of 1st qdtr group, (1ch, 1qdtr into top of same group) 4 times, *1qdtr into top of next qdtr group, (1ch, 1 qdtr into top of same group) 8 times*. Repeat from * to * another 3 (4, 5) times. 1qdtr into top of last qdtr group, (1ch, 1qdtr into top of same qdtr group) 4 times, turn.

Row 20 (23, 26) 3ch, *1dtr into next ch space, 1ch, 1trtr into next ch space, 1ch, 1qdtr into next ch space, 1ch, 1qdtr into next ch space, 1ch, 1trtr into next ch space, 1ch, 1dtr, 1ch, 1tr into next ch space, 1ch, 1tr into next ch space, 1ch*, rep from * to * to end.

Row 21 (24, 27) Make 6ch. Working into each of the next 3ch spaces, make a 3qdtr group, *7ch, 1dc into next ch space (between the 2 qdtrs), 7ch, 1qdtr into each of the next 7ch spaces (making a qdtr group)*, rep from * to * 3 (4, 5) times, 1qdtr into each of the last 4ch spaces (making a 4qdtr group), turn.

Repeat Rows 19 and 20.

Row 24 (27, 30): create strap Make 6ch. Working into each of the next 3ch spaces, make a 3qdtr group, 7ch, 1dc into next ch space, 7ch; working into the next 4ch spaces, work a qdtr group. Turn.

Row 25 (28, 31) Make 6ch, 1qdtr into top of 1st qdtr group, (1ch, 1qdtr into top of same qdtr group) 4 times. 1qdtr into top of next qdtr group, (1ch, 1qdtr into top of same qdtr group) 4 times, turn.

Row 26 (29, 34) Make 3ch, miss 1qdtr, 1dtr into next ch space, 1ch, 1trtr into next ch space, 1ch, 1qdtr into next ch space (miss 2qdtr), 1qdtr into next ch space (miss 1qdtr), 1ch, 1trtr into next ch space (miss 1qdtr), 1ch, 1tr into next ch space (miss 1qdtr). Fasten off and finish ends into piece.

Repeat the last three rows on the other edge to create the other strap.

FRONT

Make as for back until you reach Row 18.

Row 18 (21, 24): Shape armhole 1ss into each of next 8sts, 18ch, *1qdtr into next 7ch spaces (making a 7qdtr group), 7ch, 1dc into next ch space, 7ch*, repeat from * to * another 4 (5, 6) times, 1qdtr into each of last 8ch spaces, turn.

Row 19 (22, 25) Make 18ch, 1dc through ch space next to end of last row, 1ch into last 10ch, 1ch, 1qdtr into top of qdtr group, (1ch, 1qdtr into top of 1qdtr group) 8 times. Repeat qdtr group another 4 (5, 6) times. Turn.

finishing If desired, work a picot edge around the lower, neck and armhole edges of the garment.

Row 20 (23, 26) Make 6ch, *miss 1dc, 1qdtr into next dc, 1ch, miss 1dc), 1trtr into next dc, 1ch, miss 1dc), 1dtr into next dc, 1ch, miss 1dc, 1tr into next dc, 1ch, miss 1dc, 1tr into next dc, 1ch, miss 1dc, 1dtr into next dc, 1ch, miss 1dc, 1trtr into next dc, 1ch, miss 1dc, 1qdtr into next dc, 1ch*, repeat from * to * to end, turn.

Row 21 (24, 27): Create strap Make 18ch, 1qdtr into each of the next 7ch spaces (making a qdtr group), 7ch, 1dc into next ch space, turn.

Row 22 (25, 28) Make 18ch, 1dc through ch space next to end of last row, 1ss into each of next 10ch, 1ch, 1qdtr into top of 1qdtr group, (1ch, 1qdtr into top of 1qdtr group) 8 times, turn.

Row 23 (26, 29) Make 6ch, miss 1dc, 1qdtr into next dc, 1ch, miss 1dc, 1trtr into next dc, 1ch, miss 1dc, 1dtr into next dc, 1ch, miss 1dc, 1tr into next dc, 1ch, miss 1dc, 1tr into next dc, 1ch, miss 1dc, 1dtr into next dc, 1ch, miss 1dc, 1trtr into next dc, 1ch, miss 1dc, 1qdtr into next dc, 1ch, turn.

Repeat the last three rows once.

Repeat the last six rows at the opposite end of the work for the other strap. Fasten off and finish the ends into piece.

ASSEMBLY
Stitch the two pieces together at the shoulders and side seams. Finish yarn ends into the piece.

PICOT EDGING (OPTIONAL)
Join the yarn to the edge of the garment, With right side facing, work edging thus: (1dc into each of next 3 sts, 3ch, 1dc into same st as previous dc), rep to end.

Lace hat and scarf

Lacy loops of soft mohair yarn in wintry blues and greys make a feminine ensemble. Settled on the head and shoulders like a light snowfall, these pretty accessories will keep the seasonal chill away.

The narrow scarf is long enough to wrap snugly around any neck, while the cosy hat can be made in three sizes.

Materials
Artyarn Kid Mohair (70% mohair, 30% silk); 50 g (1¾ oz) ball for each of hat and scarf

Tools
4 mm (US 5/UK 8) crochet hook

Sizes
Hat instructions are given for three sizes.
- S: to fit head circumference approximately 50 cm (20 in)
- M: to fit head circumference approximately 55 cm (22 in)
- L: to fit head circumference approximately 60 cm (24 in)

The scarf is one size fits all, and measures approximately 100 x 16 cm (39½ x 6¼ in)

Tension
For the scarf, tension is not crucial.
For the hat, 17 sts and 8 rows over pattern = 10 cm (4 in)

Abbreviations
ch: chain
dc: double crochet
dtr: double treble
ss: slip stitch

hat, round 2 Work in a circle for the crown.

hat, round 4 Work lacy loops around the crown.

Hint

Tie a coloured thread onto one side of the crown of the hat, so that you can easily see which is the inside and which direction you are working in.

Hat

Make 5 (6, 7)ch, join with ss to form a ring.

Round 1 Make 6ch (counts as 1dtr and 3ch), *1dtr into ring, 3ch*, rep from * to * to end [6 (7, 8) sts]. Join with ss into 3rd of 6ch at beg of rnd.

Round 2 Make 1ch, *1dc in next ch, 3ch*, rep from * to* another 7 (8, 9) times [8, (9, 10) loops]. Join with ss into beg of rnd.

Round 3 *8ch, 1ss into next ch loop*, rep from * to * another 7 (8, 9) times [8 (9, 10) loops].

Round 4 Slip stitch across to middle of next ch loop (4ss), *8ch, 1ss into next ch loop*, rep from * to * another 7 (8, 9) times [8 (9, 10) loops].

Repeat Round 4 for size L only.

Round 5 (5, 6) Slip stitch across to middle of next ch loop (4ss), *5ch, 1ss into next ch loop*, rep from * to * to end, 1ss into ss at beg of round [48 (54, 60) ch].

Round 6 (6, 7) As for Round 2 [48 (54, 60) dc].

Round 7 (7, 8) As for Round 3 [16 (18, 20) loops].

Round 8 (8, 9) As for Round 4.

Round 9 (9, 10) As for Round 4 [16 (18, 20) loops].

Round 10 (10, 11) As for Round 5 [(96, 108, 120) ch].

scarf, row 1 The scarf begins with a row of double crochet.

scarf, step 2–6 The fabric is formed from rows of lacy loops separated by a row of double crochet.

Rounds 11 (11, 12)–14 (14, 15) Repeat Rounds 7 (7, 8)–10 (10, 11).

Round 15 (15, 16) Slip stitch across to middle of next ch loop (4ss), *4ch, 1ss into next ch loop*, rep from * to * to end, 1ss into top of 4ch at beg of rnd [80, (90, 100) ch]. Finish ends into work.

Scarf

Make 28ch, turn.

Row 1 Miss 1ch, 1dc in each ch to end, turn.

Row 2 Make 7ch, 1ss into 3rd dc, *8ch, miss 5dc, 1ss into next dc*, rep from * to * to end, turn.

Row 3 Make 7ch, 1ss into top of next ch loop, *8ch, 1ss into top of next ch loop*, rep from * to * to end, turn.

Row 4 As for Row 3.

Row 5 Make 5ch, 1ss into top of first ch loop, *5ch, 1ss into top of next ch loop*, rep from * to * to end, turn.

Row 6 Make 1ch, skip 1st ch, 1dc in each dc to end, turn.

Repeat Rows 2 to 6 another 17 times. Finish ends into work.

Concealing yarn ends

The term 'finish ends into work' means to hide the tails of yarn at the beginning and end of the work, or at the point where new yarn has been joined in, by darning them into the crocheted fabric. To do this, thread a blunt-ended needle with the tail of yarn and weave it through a few stitches on the wrong side of the work, then cut off the rest of the tail close to the surface of the fabric.

Lace skirt

This pretty skirt incorporates flower and
snowflake motifs linked by loops of lacy chain
in rich yarn colours, making this the perfect
trans-seasonal garment.

Choose a sumptuous, shiny fabric for the
underskirt to add a touch of glamour.

Materials
Rowan Soft 100 per cent merino 4-ply yarn:
   100 g (3½ oz) each of Colour 1 and Colour 2
Coloured slip or underskirt

Tools
3 mm (US 2/UK 11) crochet hook

Sizes
To fit waist size:
   S: 74 cm (29 in)
   M: 81 cm (2 in)
   L: 88 cm (34½ in)
Length approximately 70 cm (27½ in)

Tension (after blocking)
Small 5-petal flower = 6 cm (2½ in) diameter
Medium 5-petal flower = 8 cm (3¼ in) diameter
Large 8-petal flower = 10 cm (4 in) diameter
Snowflake = 14 cm (5½ in) from picot to picot

Abbreviations
ch: chain
dc: double crochet
qdtr: quadruple treble
ss: slip stitch
tr: treble
trtr: triple treble

snowflake Work in Colour 1.

small five-petal flower Work in Colour 1.

SNOWFLAKE Make 10 (11, 12)

Using Colour 1, make 9ch, join with ss to form a ring.

Round 1 Make 8ch, *3tr into ring, 5ch*, rep from * to * 4 times, 2tr into ring, 1ss into 3rd of 8ch at beg of rnd.

Round 2 1ss into 1st ch, 7ch, 4tr into ch loop, *miss 3tr, 1ch, 4tr into ch loop, 4ch, 4tr into ch loop*, rep from * to * 4 times, 1ch, 3tr into ch loop, 1ss into 3rd of 7ch at beg of rnd.

Round 3 1ss into each of next 2ch, 6ch, 3tr into ch loop (miss 4tr, 1ch, 4tr), *3ch, 3tr into ch loop, 3ch, 3tr into ch loop*, rep from * to * 4 times, 3ch, 2tr into ch loop, 1ss into 3rd of 6ch at beg of rnd.

Round 4 1ss into each of next 2ch, 8ch, 1ss into same place as previous ss (making a 4-ch picot), 1ch, 2tr into ch loop, (miss 3tr, 1ch), *5ch, 1dc around 1ch, (miss 1ch, 3tr), 5ch, 2tr into ch loop, 5ch, 1ss into 4ch, 1ch, 2tr into ch loop*, rep from * to * 4 times, (miss 3tr, 1ch), 5ch, 1dc around 1ch (miss 1ch, 3tr), 5ch, 1tr into ch loop, 1ss into 3rd of 8ch at beg of rnd. Fasten off.

SMALL FIVE-PETAL FLOWER Make 10 (11, 12)

Using Colour 1, make 4ch, join with ss to form a ring.

Round 1 5ch, *1tr into ring, 2ch*, rep from * to * 3 times, 1ss into 3rd of 5ch at beg of rnd.

medium five-petal flower Work in Colour 1.

large eight-petal flower Work in Colour 1.

Round 2 *5ch, 3trtr group into ch space, 5ch, 1dc into next tr*, rep from * to * four times. Fasten off.

MEDIUM FIVE-PETAL FLOWER
Make 10 (11, 12) Using Colour 1, make 4ch, join with ss to form a ring.
Round 1 Make 5ch, *1tr into ring, 2ch*, rep from * to * 3 times, 1ss into 3rd of 5ch at beg of rnd.
Round 2 1ch, 1dc into each st to end, 1ss into 1st ch of rnd.
Round 3 *Make 7ch. Working into each of the next 3 sts, make a 3qdtr group, 7ch, 1dc into same st as last qdtr of group*, rep from * to * four times. Fasten off.

LARGE EIGHT-PETAL FLOWER
Make 10 (11, 12)
Using Colour 1, make 6ch, join with ss to form a ring.
Round 1 Make 1ch, 12dc into ring.
Round 2 Make 2ch, 2tr into each dc to end, 1ss into top of 2ch at beg of rnd.
Round 3 *Make 7ch. Working into each of the next 3 sts, make a 3qdtr group, 7ch, 1dc into same st as last qdtr of group*, rep from * to * seven times. Fasten off.

Finish yarn ends into all motifs. Press all of the flowers and snowflakes to size, taking care not to distort their shape.

Hint

Make this skirt in larger sizes by increasing the waistband in 7 cm (2¾ in) increments. Make one extra of each motif for each 7 cm (2¾ in) increase.

WAISTBAND

Using Colour 2, make 6ch, turn.

Round 1 Make 1ch, miss 1st ch, 1dc into each ch to end, turn.

Round 2 Make 1ch, miss 1st ch, 1dc into each dc to end, turn.

Repeat Row 2 until waistband measures 77 (84, 91) cm, or length required if making a larger size (see Hint, page 41). Stitch the two ends together to make a loop, being careful not to twist the waistband.

ASSEMBLING THE MOTIFS

Join Colour 2 to waistband. Working in rounds, complete the skirt from the top down to the bottom.

Round 1 *Make 8ch, 1dc into top edge of small flower side petal, 8ch, 1dc into waistband (2.5cm/1 in along waistband), 5ch, 1dc into top of next petal, 5ch, 1dc into waistband (2.5cm/1 in along waistband), 8ch, 1dc into top edge of next side petal, 8ch, 1dc into waistband (2.5cm/1 in along waistband)*, rep from * to * to join all of the small flowers to the skirt.

Round 2 Make 33ch, 1dc into bottom petal on small flower, 7ch, 1dc into last petal, 15ch*, rep from * to * to end, 7ch, 1ss through 26th ch on 1st loop.

Round 3 1dc into each st until 1 st rem, miss last st, 1ss into 1st dc of rnd.

Round 4 Make 17ch, miss 14dc, *1dc into next dc (to align between two lower petals of small flower above), 17ch, miss 14dc, 1dc into next dc (to align between two small flowers above)*, rep from * to * to end, 1ss through base of 17ch at beg of rnd.

Round 5 1ss into each of next 8ch, *17ch, 1dc into next ch loop*, rep from * to * to end, 1ss into ch above 8th ss at beg of rnd.

Round 6 1ss into each of next 8ch, *10ch, 1dc into next ch loop*, rep from * to * to end, join with ss to beg of rnd.

Round 7 1ch, 1dc into each ch to end, join with ss to beg of round.

Round 8 *10ch, 1dc into top edge of medium flower side petal; 10ch, miss 7dc, 1dc into next dc, 7ch, 1dc into top of next petal, 7ch, miss 6dc, 1dc into next dc, 10ch, 1dc into top edge of next side petal; 10ch, miss 7dc, 1dc into next dc*, rep from * to * to join all of the medium flowers around the skirt. Join with ss to 1st ch of rnd.

Round 9 45ch, *1dc into bottom petal of medium flower, 20ch, 1dc into last petal, 20ch*, rep from * to * to end, 10ch, join with ss into 35th ch at beg of rnd.

Round 10 1ch, 1dc into each ch to end, join with ss into 1st ch of rnd.

Round 11 *20ch, miss 19dc, 1dc into next dc (to align between lower two petals of flower above)*, rep from * to * to end, join with ss into 1st ch of rnd.

Round 12 1ss into each of next 10ch, *20ch, miss 19ch, 1dc into next dc*, rep from * to * to end, 1ss into ch above the last ss at beg of rnd.

Round 13 1ss into each of next 10ch, *12ch, 1dc into next ch loop*, rep from * to * to end, 1ss into 1st ss of rnd.

Round 14 1ch, 1dc into each ch to end, 1ss into 1st ch of rnd.

Round 15 *Make 15ch, 1dc into the top edge of large flower side petal, 15ch, miss 5dc, 1dc into next dc, 10ch, 1dc into the top of next petal, 10ch, miss 5dc, 1dc into next dc, 10dc, 1dc into the top of next petal, 10ch, miss 5dc, 1dc into next dc, 15ch, 1dc into the edge of next side petal, 15ch, miss 5dc, 1dc into next dc*, rep from * to * to join all of the large flowers.

Round 16 Make 55ch, *1dc into bottom

waistband Work in double crochet in Colour 2 until the required length is reached.

assembly, round 19 Join the motifs in rounds using chain stitch filigree and bands of double crochet in Colour 2.

edge of side petal on large flower, 25ch, 1dc into bottom of next petal, 20ch, 1dc into bottom of next petal, 25ch, 1dc into bottom edge of next side petal, 30ch*, rep from * to * to end, 15ch, join with ss into 40th of 50ch at beg of rnd.

Round 17 *Make 6ch, 1dc into next ch loop,* rep from * to * to end, join with ss into 1st ch of rnd.

Round 18 1ch, 1dc into each ch to end, 1ss into 1st ch of rnd.

Round 19 Working backwards along previous round, make 1ss into each of first 3dc. Then, moving forward, *make 25ch, 1dc through side picot of two snowflakes together, 25ch, miss 2dc, 1dc into next dc,

3dc, 10ch, 1dc through next picot on snowflake, 10ch, miss 6dc, 1dc into next dc, 12ch; miss 2tr and 5ch on snowflake, 1dc into central dc on side of snowflake, 12ch, miss 6dc, 1dc into next dc, 10ch, 1dc into next picot on snowflake, 10ch, miss 6dc, 1dc into next dc, 25ch, 1dc through next picot on this snowflake and side picot on next snowflake together*, rep from * to * to join all of the snowflakes to the skirt. Fasten off and finish yarn ends into piece.

Hint

Rather than stitch the silky lining slip to the skirt, choose or make a selection of coloured slips to give your crochet work different flavours for your various moods.

Beaded lace bag

A lacy, crocheted overlay scattered with beads turns a simple bag into something special. Crushed velvet makes the handbag suitable for stylish day or glamorous evening wear.

Beads are easily incorporated into crocheted fabric. First, thread all of the beads onto the yarn or thread, or — if the yarn or thread is too thick to pass through the holes of the beads — onto a piece of nylon filament (invisible thread). This is the method used in this project. The filament is then crocheted alongside the main yarn. As you reach the stitch where a bead is required, slide a bead up the yarn or filament and hold it in place while you form the stitch around it.

Materials
100 g (3½ oz) Rowan Soft 100 per cent merino 4-ply yarn
1 spool filament yarn (invisible thread)
200 assorted small to medium beads
30 cm (12 in) velvet or satin fabric
40 cm (16 in) polyester boning

Tools
3 mm (US 2/UK 11) crochet hook

Size
Approximately 25 cm (10 in) long x 22 cm (9 in) wide, not including handles

Tension
Tension is not crucial for this item

Abbreviations
b/ch: beaded chain
ch: chain
dc: double crochet
dtr: double treble
ss: slip stitch
tr: treble

lace overlay, round 8 Work double trebles into the previous row.

bag construction, step 2 Make two tubes into which the pieces of boning will be inserted to make the handles.

LACE OVERLAY

Make 90ch, join with ss to form a ring.

Round 1 1dc into each ch to end, join with ss to 1st ch of round.

Round 2 1dc into 1st dc, * 3ch, miss 3dc, 1dc into each of next 3dc*, rep from * to * to end, 1ss into 1st ch of rnd.

Round 3 1ch, *5tr in next ch loop, miss 1dc, 1dc in the next dc, miss 1dc*, rep from * to * to end, 1ss into 1st ch of rnd.

Round 4 1ch, miss 1tr, 1dc into each of the next 3tr, *3ch, miss 3 sts, 1dc into each of next 3tr*, rep from * to * to end, 1ss into 1st ch of rnd.

Round 5 Miss 1dc, 1dc into next dc, miss 1dc, *5tr in the next 3ch space, miss 1dc, 1dc in next dc*, rep from * to * to end, 1ss into 1st dc of rnd, 1ss into space in first 3tr.

Round 6 4ch, miss 2 sts, 1dc into each of next 3tr, * 4ch, miss 3 sts, 1dc into each of next 3tr*, rep from * to * to end, 1ss into 1st of 4ch at beg of rnd.

Round 7 3ch, *(1dtr into next 4ch space, 1ch) 4 times, 1tr in next dc, 2tr in next dc, 1tr in next dc, 1ch*, rep from * to * to end, 1ss into top of 3ch at beg of rnd.

Round 8 3ch, *(1dtr into next dtr, 1dtr into next ch space) 3 times, 1dtr into next dtr; working into the next 2dtr, make a 2dtr group, (miss the top of the tr group)*, rep from * to * to end, 1ss into top of 3ch at beg of rnd.

Round 9 3ch, 1tr into 1st dtr, 1ch, *1dtr into next dtr, 1ch, 1dtr into next dtr, 1ch, 1dtr into next dtr, 1ch, 1dtr into next dtr, 1ch, 1tr into each of next 3dtr, 1ch*, rep from * to * to end, 1ss into top of 3ch at beg of rnd.

Round 10 1ch, *1ch into 1st tr, 1ss into next ch, 1ch into next dtr, 1ss into next ch, 1ch into next dtr, 1ss into next ch, make 4-ch picot, 1ch into next dtr, 1ss into next ch, 1ch into next dtr*, rep from * to * to end, 1ss into 1st ch of rnd.

Round 11 *15ch, (miss 4ch, 1picot, 5ch), 1ss into next ch*, rep from * to * to end, 1ss into 1st of 15ch at beg of rnd.

Round 12 *1dc into each of first 7ch, make three 4-ch picots into next ch, 1dc into each of next 7ch*, rep from * to * to end, 1ss into 1st dc of rnd.

Round 13 1ss into each of next 7dc, 1ss into 1st picot, 1ss into 2nd picot, *10ch, 1ss into central picot of next group*, rep from * to * to end, 1ss into top of slip sts at beg of rnd.

Rounds 14–16 Repeat Rounds 10–12.

BEADING

Thread 200 beads onto filament yarn, and run the filament alongside the crochet yarn.

Round 17 1ss into each of the first 7dc and into first 2 picots, *3ch, 1b/ch, 3ch, 1b/ch, 3ch, 1b/ch, 3ch, 1ch into central picot of next group*, rep from * to * to end, join with ss to beg of rnd.

Round 18 1ss into each of first 7ch, *2ch, 1b/ch, 2ch, 1b/ch, 3ch, 1b/ch, 2ch, 1b/ch, 2ch, 1ss into centre of next ch loop*, rep from * to * to end, 1ss into 1st ch of rnd.

Round 19 1ss into each of first 7ch, 1ch, *2ch, 1b/ch, 2ch, 1b/ch, 1ch, 1b/ch, 1ch, 1b/ch, 2ch, 1b/ch, 2ch, 1ss into centre of

next ch loop*, rep from * to * to end. Fasten off.

BAG CONSTRUCTION

1 Finish all ends into the piece. Press bag carefully to remove any creases or curls.

2 Cut the polyester boning into two lengths of 20 cm (8 in) each. To make the casing for the handles, make 90ch, turn, *1ch, 1dc into each ch to end, turn*, rep from * to * 3 times. Fold the long edges together, with wrong sides facing, and form into a tube by crocheting the two long edges together using dc. Repeat to make a second tube, then slide a piece of polyester boning inside each to make the bag handles.

3 Using the pattern in Diagram 1, cut two pieces each of bag fabric and lining fabric; overlock or hem edges. Pin two bag pieces with right sides together, and stitch down each side and across the bottom, then fold bottom corners together and stitch across. Trim off ends and turn right side out.

4 Pin the lining pieces with the right sides together, and stitch down each side. Stitch the ends of the bottom edge, leaving a gap of about 10 (4 in) cm for turning through. Fold the bottom corners together and stitch across. Trim ends and leave wrong side out.

5 Pin the top edge of the crochet bag to the outside top edge of the fabric bag. Pin the handles in place (facing the wrong way up) on the outside of the bag, then pin the lining bag (with the wrong side facing out), to the right side of the two other pieces. Stitch around the top edge of the bag. Trim off the ends.

6 Turn the lining to the right side and stitch the seam closed along the bottom, then tuck the lining inside the bag and press the top edge.

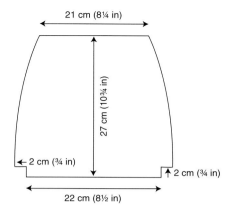

diagram 1 **Bag and lining** Cut 2 pieces in each of bag fabric and lining fabric. Before cutting, measure the crocheted overlay and adjust the above measurements if necessary.

Hints

Contrast fabric will help emphasize the crochet, and contrasting beads will add extra interest.

Alternative yarns could be incorporated at different stages in the crochet to give a striped effect with each round.

Try beaded chains instead of crochet handles to give a glamorous look for evening.

To make a smaller or larger bag, reduce or increase the initial chain by increments of 12, and alter the size of the fabric bag accordingly.

Beaded choker and cuff

This delicate choker and cuff set, encrusted with

pearly beads and crystals, will add the perfect

finishing touch to a chic evening ensemble.

Made in white or off-white, as here, it would be

a lovely adornment for a bridal outfit.

Fine rayon yarn has a lustre that complements

the beads, giving an elegant touch. Substitute

silk or silk/rayon blends for a different look.

If you have not crocheted with beads before,

see page 44 for an explanation of the technique.

Materials
50 g (1¾ oz) ball Sullivans Royal Rayon 3-ply
   crochet yarn (one ball of yarn is enough to
   make both the choker and the cuff)
286 assorted small beads (choker)
147 assorted small beads (cuff)
Four 6 mm (¼ in) pearl buttons (two each for
   choker and cuff)

Tools
1 mm (US 11 or 12/UK 6 or 5½) crochet hook

Size
Choker: 32 x 5 cm (12¾ x 2 in), not including
   beaded loops
Cuff: 17 x 5 cm (6½ x 5 cm), not including
   beaded loops

Tension
1 row qdtr and 3 rows dc in patt across 21ch
   = 5 cm (2 in) wide x 3 cm (1¼ in) deep

Abbreviations
b/ch: beaded chain
b/dc: beaded double crochet
ch: chain
dc: double crochet
qdtr: quadruple treble
ss: slip stitch

Choker

BEADED CROCHET

String 220 beads onto the yarn. Make 21ch.

Row 1 Miss 1ch, 1dc in next of next 20ch, turn.

Rows 2–4 As for Row 1.

Row 5 Make 1ch, miss 1dc, *1dc in next dc, 1b/dc in next dc*, rep from * to * to end, turn.

Row 6 Make 1ch, miss 1dc, 1dc in each of next 20dc, turn.

Row 7 As for Row 5.

Row 8 Make 5ch, *1qdtr in 1st dc, 1ch, miss 1dc, 1qdtr in next dc, 1ch*, rep from * to * to end, turn.

Repeat Rows 5–8 another 9 times.

Repeat Rows 5–6.

Repeat Row 1 twice.

Next row: Make button loops Make 1ch, miss 1dc, 1dc in each of next 5dc, 12ch, 1dc in each of next 10dc, 12ch, 1dc in each of next 5ch, cut off yarn. Finish ends into work.

FINISHING

1 Sew the buttons onto the other end of the choker, aligning them opposite the button loops, to create fastenings.

2 String 30 beads onto the yarn. Join the yarn to the choker (at beginning of work) using 1ss. *(3ch, 1b/ch) 3 times, 3ch, then use 1ss to attach work between the first and second rows of quadruple treble*, rep from * to * to end [10 loops]. Finish ends into work.

3 String 36 beads onto the yarn. Join the yarn to the centre of the first loop that you made in step 2, using 1ss. *(3ch, 1b/ch) 4 times, 3ch, then use 1ss to attach work to centre of the next loop of the previous row*, rep from * to * to end [9 loops]. Finish ends into work.

Cuff

BEADED CROCHET

String 120 beads onto the yarn. Make 21ch.

Row 1 Miss 1ch, 1dc in each of next 20ch, turn.

Rows 2–4 As for Row 1.

beaded yarn Thread beads onto the yarn before beginning the crochet.

Row 5 Make 1ch, miss 1dc, *1dc in next dc, 1b/dc in next dc*, rep from * to * to end, turn.

Row 6 Make 1ch, miss 1dc, 1dc in each of next 20dc, turn.

Row 7 As for Row 6.

Row 8 Make 5ch, *1qdtr in 1st dc, 1ch, miss 1dc, 1qdtr in next dc, 1ch*, rep from * to * to end, turn.

Repeat Rows 5–8 another 4 times.

Repeat Rows 5–6.

Repeat Row 1 twice.

Row 29: Make button loops Make 1ch, miss 1dc, 1dc in each of next 5dc, 12ch, 1dc in each of next 10dc, 12ch, 1dc in each of next 5ch, cut off yarn. Finish ends into work.

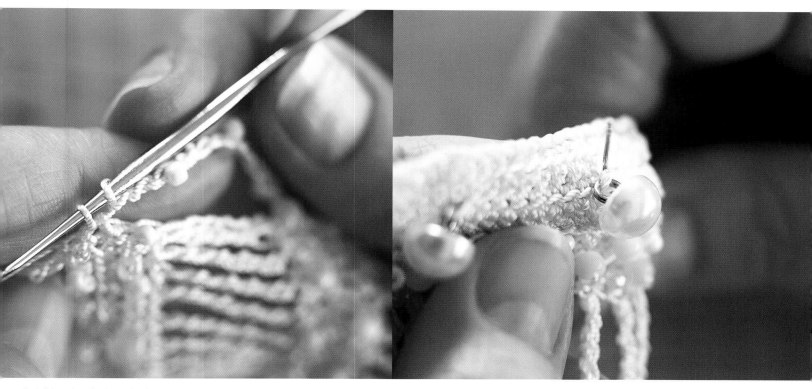

crochet Move beads along the thread when beaded stitches are indicated.

choker, finishing, step 1 Sew buttons onto one end of the choker, aligning them opposite the button loops.

FINISHING

1 Sew the buttons onto the other end of the cuff, aligning them opposite the button loops, to create fastenings.
2 String 15 beads onto the yarn. Join the yarn to the cuff (at beginning of work) using 1ss. *(3ch, 1b/ch) 3 times, 3ch, then use 1ss to fix work between first and second rows of quadruple trebles*, rep from * to * to end [5 loops]. Finish ends into work.
3 String 12 beads onto the yarn. Join the yarn to the centre of the first loop you made in step 2, using 1ss. *(3ch, 1b/ch) 3 times, 3ch, then use 1ss to fix work to centre of the second loop of the previous row*, rep from * to * to end [4 loops]. Finish ends into work.

Hints

To make the cuff or choker larger, add repeats of Rows 5 to 8.
To make the cuff or choker smaller, remove repeats of Rows 5 to 8.

Steps 2 and 3 of Finishing (the beaded loop sections) can be omitted to give a simpler effect.

To use smaller beads which will not thread onto the yarn, thread the beads onto a nylon filament (invisible thread) and crochet this alongside the main yarn.

Any smooth 3-ply yarn can be used for these designs. To use a textured yarn, thread the beads onto a filament and crochet alongside the main yarn. Lurex thread can also be crocheted alongside the main yarn to give a different look.

Table runner

Give a table or dresser a retro look with this table runner. With its hippie-style bobbles draped over the edge, it will add groove to your table setting.

Double-knit cotton yarn is practical and hard-wearing, and washable in case of spills and drips.

Materials
100 g (3½ oz) Rowan Handknit Cotton double-knit (8-ply) yarn in each of Colour 1 and Colour 2
Small bag of polyester fibrefill

Tools
3 mm (US 2/UK 11) crochet hook

Size
Approximately 100 x 20 cm (39 x 8 in), not including bobble fringe

Tension
20 sts and 11 rows over pattern = 10 cm (4 in)

Abbreviations
ch: chain
dc: double crochet
dtr: double treble
qtr: quadruple treble
ss: slip stitch
tr: treble

runner Two colours are alternated throughout the piece.

RUNNER

Using Colour 1, make 202ch, turn.

Row 1 Miss 1ch, 1dc into each ch to end, turn.

Row 2 6ch, miss 1dc, *1qdtr into next st, 1ch, miss 1st*, rep from * to * to end, 1qdtr into last st, turn.

Row 3 1ch, 1dc into each st to end, turn.

Row 4 As for Row 3.

Row 5 Using Colour 2, as for Row 3.

Row 6 3ch, 1tr into each st to end, turn.

Row 7 1ch, 1dc into each st to end, turn.

Rows 8–9 Using Colour 1, as for Row 3.

Row 10 Using Colour 2, as for Row 3.

Row 11 3ch, miss 1dc, *1dtr into next st, 1ch, miss 1st*, rep from * to * to end, 1 dtr

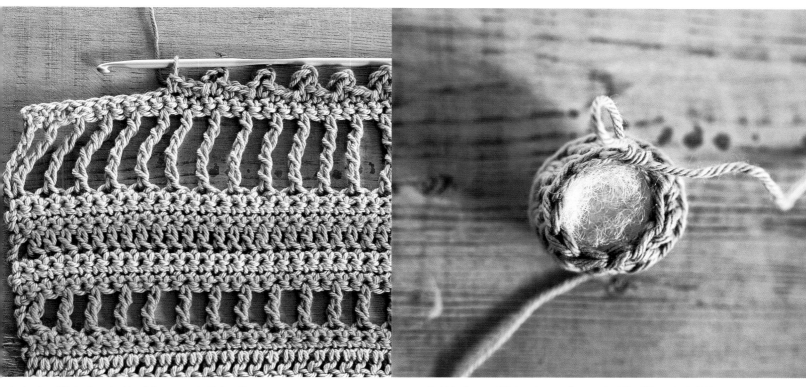

picot edge Work at each side of the runner in Colour 2.

bobble 1, round 5 Insert a small amount of fibrefill into the bobble.

into last st, turn.

Row 12 Make 1ch, 1dc into each st to end, turn.

Using Colour 1, rep Row 3, then Row 6.

Using Colour 2, rep Row 7, then Row 2, then Row 3.

Using Colour 1, rep Row 3, then Row 6.

Using Colour 2, rep Row 7, then Row 11, then Row 12.

Using Colour 1, rep Row 3 twice.

Using Colour 2, rep Row 3, then row 6, then row 7.

Using Colour 1, rep Row 3 twice, then Row 2, then Row 3.

Fasten off and finish ends into the piece.

PICOT EDGE

1 With the right side of the work facing, join Colour 2 to the right-hand edge of the end of the piece.

2 1ch, 1dc into each of first 2dc, *4ch, 1ss into same st as prev dc (to make 4-ch picot), 1dc into each of next 3dc*, rep from * to * to end. Fasten off, finish ends into piece.

3 Repeat Steps 1 and 2 for the other edge of the piece.

BOBBLE 1 Make 16 (8 of Colour 1, 8 of Colour 2)

Round 1 Make 2ch, 7dc into 1st ch to make a small disc.

Round 2 2ch into each dc to end.

tails, step 1 Work in double crochet back down the length of the chain.

tails, step 2 Attach one large and one small bobble to each tail.

Round 3 1ss into each st to end.

Round 4 1dc into each st to end.

Round 5 1dc into each st to end.

Fill bobble with a small amount of polyester fibrefill.

Round 6 1ss into next dc, *skip 1dc, 1ss into next dc (to decrease)*, rep from * to * to end.

Round 7 As for Round 6.

Feed end of yarn through ch at top of bobble, pull tight and fasten off. Finish ends into bobble.

BOBBLE 2 Make 16 (8 of Colour 1, 8 of Colour 2)

Round 1 2ch, 5dc into 1st ch to make a small disc.

Round 2 2ss into each st to end.

Round 3 1ss into each st to end.

Round 4 1dc into each st to end.

Fill bobble with a small amount of polyester fibrefill.

Round 5 1ss into next dc, *skip 1dc, 1ss into next dc (to decrease)*, rep from * to * to end.

Round 6 As for Round 5.

Feed end of yarn through ch at top of bobble, pull tight and fasten off. Finish ends into bobble.

tails, step 3 When attaching bobbles, match the bobble colour to that of the tail.

TAILS

1 Using Colour 2, make 70ch. Make 2dc through the end of the runner at the short edge, make 1dc into each of the next 50ch (working back down the tail), make 10ch, fasten off.

2 Using the end of yarn on the longer end of the tail, stitch a large bobble onto the tail. Using the other end of yarn at the shorter end of the tail, stitch on a smaller bobble.

3 Create eight tails of varying lengths along either end of the runner, matching the colours to those of the runner at the point where you attach the tails. Work tails of 70ch, 60ch, 50ch and 40ch, working back 50ch, 40ch, 30ch, 20ch respectively, and finishing each tail with 10ch as in Step 1. Repeat Step 2 to attach two bobbles to each tail.

Hint

For placemats to match, crochet the same repeat on a shorter base of 50ch, working the picot edge all the way around and not adding bobbles.

Beaded door curtain

Light plays on the beads that serve both practical and decorative purposes for this shimmering item of décor. As a pretty cover-up for a doorway, this curtain will add a touch of fantasy to a room's entrance, while the movement of the beads will also serve to keep insects out.

Glass beads of various sizes work as weights to keep the crocheted strands from tangling together in the breeze. The strings of beads are attached at the top via a fabric pocket to a length of dowel, which can be suspended via cup hooks or other means over the doorway.

Materials
5 large spools Coats Buttonhole (bonded nylon) thread
4000 assorted medium-sized beads (the beads should be a mixture of materials, such as glass and plastic, to reduce the weight of the curtain)
10 x 84 cm (4 x 33 in) piece satin fabric
80 cm (31½ in) length of dowel

Tools
1 mm (US 11 or 12/UK 5½ or 6) crochet hook

Size
To fit standard doorway, but can be customized

Tension
Tension is not crucial for this project

Abbreviations
ch: chain
b/ch: beaded chain

beaded chains Thread a selection of beads onto the bonded nylon yarn.

step 1 Slide a bead up the yarn and work over it to create the beaded chain stitch.

BEADED CHAINS

1 String 50 beads onto the yarn. Make 2ch; (1b/ch, 4ch) five times; (1b/ch, 5ch) five times; (1b/ch, 6ch) five times; (1b/ch, 7ch) five times; (1b/ch, 8ch) five times; (1b/ch, 9ch) five times; (1b/ch, 10ch) five times; (1b/ch, 11ch) five times; (1b/ch, 12ch) five times; (1b/ch, 13ch) five times.
Work a further 200ch, or until total length measures height of door, allowing for weight of beads to cause the chain length to drop slightly; see Hint opposite. Break off yarn.
2 Repeat Step 1 another 79 times, to give 80 chains of beads.

rod pocket Make a tube of satin fabric to hold the dowel.

JOINING CHAIN LENGTHS

Make 3ch, *1ss through the top (unbeaded) end of a chain length, 3ch*, rep until all chain lengths are incorporated (the width should be 80 cm/31½ in, which is an average door width).

CREATING ROD POCKET

1 Overlock the edges of the satin fabric and press a small hem allowance on all sides. Sew the strip of chain joining all of the lengths (step 3) to the right side of one edge of the satin fabric, inside the hem allowance.

2 Fold the satin strip in half lengthwise (wrong sides together) and stitch the long edges together to form a tube. Sew one end of the tube closed, insert the dowel and close the other end.

Hang the beaded curtain from cup hooks or similar hooks fixed above the doorway.

Hints

An assortment of bead sizes will give slightly different chain lengths, which gives a more random appearance.

Fewer beads per chain will give a simpler look.

The chains may increase in length once hung for a time, so it is a good idea to hang each chain from a hook as it is completed, to allow some of the length to drop.

Glass beads are heavier and can help the chains swing better, but be careful not to use too many as this can make the whole curtain very heavy.

As alternatives to beads you could use such objects as sequins, shells or even buttons, which will give a unique style.

Smaller versions of this curtain could be made for windows.

Mohair lace wrap

Softly draped over the shoulders, this asymmetric
open-work shawl is snuggly and light to wear,
and quick to work using a large hook. Made from
a variegated mohair yarn, it features crocheted
spirals of treble stitches swirling across the edge.

Materials
125 g (4 oz) Jo Sharp Infusion Kid Mohair
    4-ply yarn

Tools
5 mm (US 7/UK 6) crochet hook

Size
One size fits most; the wrap measures
    approximately 175 x 85 cm (69 x 33½ in)

Tension
Swirl motif = 20 cm (8 inch) diameter after
    blocking

Abbreviations
ch: chain
dc: double crochet
dtr: double treble
qdtr: quadruple treble
ss: slip stitch
tr: treble
trtr: triple treble

SWIRL Make 3

Make 9ch, join with ss to form a ring.

Round 1 3ch, *1tr into ring, 2ch*, rep from * to * another 6 times, 1tr into 1st ch space.

Round 2 4ch, 1dtr into next ch space, *4ch, 1tr into next tr, 4ch, 1tr into next ch space, 4ch, 1tr into next ch space, 4ch, 1tr into next ch space*, rep from * to * once.

Round 3 4ch, 1trtr into next ch space, 4ch, 1trtr into next dtr, 4ch, 1trtr into next ch space, 4ch, 1trtr into next dtr, *4ch, 1trtr into next ch space, 4ch, 1trtr into next ch space, 4ch, 1trtr into next dtr*, rep from * to * twice.

Round 4 *4ch, 1dtr into next ch space, 4ch, 1dtr into next dtr*, rep from * to * 3 times. 4ch, 1tr into next ch space, 3ch, 1tr into next trtr, 3ch, 1tr into next ch space, 2ch, 1tr into next trtr, 2ch, 1dc into next ch space, 1ch into next ch. Fasten off, finish ends into the piece.

CRESCENT Make 2

Make 9ch, join with ss to form a ring. (Note that this shape is made in rows, not rounds.)

Row 1 3ch, 1tr into ring, *2ch, 1tr into ring*, rep from * to * 3 times, turn.

Row 2 3ch, *1tr into ch loop, 2ch, 1tr into next tr, 2ch*, rep from * to * 3 times, 1tr into last ch loop, turn.

Row 3 10ch, *1tr into next tr, 2ch, 1tr into next tr, 8ch*, rep from * to * another 3 times, 10ch, 1dc into last ch loop, turn.

Row 4 1ch, 1ss into each of first 5ch, 8ch, *1dc through next 8-ch loop, 8ch*, rep from * to * another 3 times (last dc should be through last 8-ch loop), turn.

Row 5 *10ch, 1dc into 8-ch loop, 10ch, 1dc into next dc*, rep from * to * another 3 times, turn.

Row 6 1ch, 1ss into each of first 5ch, *10ch, 1dc into next 10-ch loop*, rep from * to * another 6 times, 1ss into each of last 5ch of 8-ch loop, turn.

Row 7 1ch, 1ss into each ch to end, turn.

Row 8 1ch, 1dc into each of next 5ch, *4ch, 1ss into same st as 1st dc (making 4-ch picot), 1dc into each of next 10ch*, rep from * to * to end. Fasten off and finish ends into piece.

pomegranate Join the two halves.

POMEGRANATE Make 4

Make 5ch, join with ss to form a ring. (Note that this shape is made in rows, not rounds.)

Row 1 *10ch, 1dc into ring*, rep from * to * twice, turn.

Row 2 1ch, 1ss into each of first 5ch, (8ch, 1ss into each of middle 3ch of next 10-ch loop) twice, turn.

Row 3 1ch, 1dc into each ch to end [26dc], turn.

Row 4 12ch, *miss 4dc, 1dc into next dc, 1ss into last 4ch of 12ch just made, 8ch*, rep from * to * another 5 times, 1dc into last dc, turn.

Row 5 1ch, 1dc into each ch around entire piece, to end. Fasten off and finish ends into piece.

Joining Place two pieces with RS together and crochet along the flat edge (using ss), through both pieces, to make one large piece. Repeat with the other two pieces, to give two large pieces.

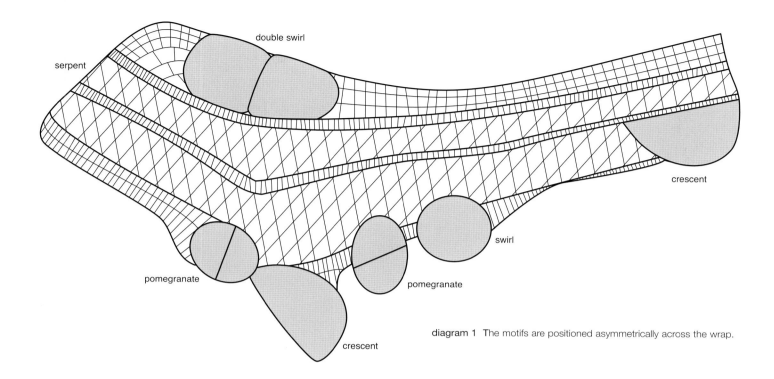

diagram 1 The motifs are positioned asymmetrically across the wrap.

BEGIN ASSEMBLY

Lightly press all pieces. Place two swirls, RS together (these will be at the top centre of the wrap).

Row 1 1ch, 1ss through each of first 10ch on both swirls, 1ss into each of next 5ch on first swirl, 6ch (miss 8ch on second swirl), 1ss into each of 9ch on second swirl. 10ch (miss 6ch on first swirl), 1ss into each of 7ch on first swirl, 1dc into each ch entire way around first swirl.

Row 2 1ss into each of the first 5ch on second swirl, 6ch (miss 8dc on first swirl), 1ss into each of 9dc on first swirl. 10ch (miss 6ch on second swirl), 1ss into each of 7ch on second swirl, 1dc into each ch around second swirl to end, fasten off and fix ends into piece.

SERPENT Make 1

Row 1 78ch, 1dc through dc at one o'clock point on double swirl, 1dc into each dc along the top edge of the double swirl (40dc), 40ch, turn.

Row 2 1ch, 1dc into each ch to end, turn.

Row 3 3ch; (1dtr into next dc, 1ch, miss 1dc) 41 times; (1dtr into next dc, 2 ch, miss 1dc) eight times; (1dtr into next dc, 1ch, miss 1dc) 30 times; 1dtr into last dc, turn.

Row 4 8ch, 1dc into 2nd ch sp; (10ch, miss 2dtr, 1dc into next dtr) 11 times; (12ch, miss 2dtr, 1dc into next dtr) three times; (10ch, miss 2dtr, 1dc into next dtr) 14 times, turn.

Row 5 14ch, 1dc into next ch loop; (10ch, 1dc into next ch loop) 15 times; 12ch, 1dc into next ch loop, (12ch, 1dc into next ch loop) three times; (10ch, 1dc into next ch loop) nine times; 1dc into 4ch of last ch loop, turn.

Row 6 14ch, 1dc into next ch loop; (10ch, 1dc into next ch loop) 9 times; (12ch, 1dc into next ch loop) three times; (10ch, 1dc into next ch loop) to end, turn.

Row 7 10ch, 1dc into ch loop; (7ch, 1dc into next ch loop) 15 times; (10ch, 1dc into next ch loop) four times; (7ch, 1dc into next ch loop) nine times; turn.

Row 8 3ch, *(1dtr into next ch, miss 1ch)* 37 times; (1dtr into next ch, 2ch, miss 1ch) 16 times, rep from * to * to end, 1 dtr into last st, turn.

Row 9 1ch, 1dc into each st to end, turn.

Row 10 1ch, 1st into each st to end, fasten off and finish ends into piece.

CONSTRUCTING THE MAIN FABRIC

Refer to Diagram 1 on previous page. Right side, short end of the serpent should be facing you.

Row 1 Make 1ch, 1ss through the 30th ch in on first edge at short end of serpent (this is the right-hand end with the swirls towards you), 1ss into each of the next 4ch (towards swirls), 3ch, 1ss into each of the next 6ch on swirl (away from join), 1ss into each of the next 6ch, 7ch, 1ss into first ch on serpent, turn.

Row 2 1ss into each of the next 9ch (away from join), 12ch, 1dc around last link between serpent and double swirl, 1ss into each of the next 7ch back up away from dc, 1ss into each of the next 7ch on swirl, turn.

Row 3 *12ch, 1dc into last loop, 1ss into each of last 7ch*, rep from * to * again, 6ch, 1dc into each of 7ch along swirl, turn.

Row 4 1ch, 1dc into each st to end, turn.

Row 5 1ss into each of the next 8ch, 3ch, miss 1dc, *1qdtr into next dc, miss 1dc, 3ch*, rep from * to * three times, **1qdtr into next dc, miss 1dc, 2ch**, rep from ** to ** four times, 2ch, 1dc into each of next 8ch on serpent, turn.

Row 6 1ss into each of next 8ch, *2ch, miss 1st, 1qdtr into next st*, rep from * to * four times, **3ch, miss 1ch, 1qdtr into next st**, rep from ** to ** three times, 3ch, 1dc into each of next 6ch on swirl, turn.

Row 7 1ch, 1dc into each st to end, turn.

Row 8 1ch, 1dc into each st to end, fasten off and finish ends into piece.

JOINING CRESCENTS

With right sides facing, place one crescent with the point at the long end of the serpent, flat edge to the outer edge of serpent and right sides together.

Row 1 1ch, ss along the edges to join them together. At the end of the crescent, work *10ch, miss 6ch, 1dc into next ch*, rep from * to * to end, turn.

Row 2 12ch, 1dc into next ch loop, *10ch, 1dc into next ch loop*, rep from * to * to end, 12ch, miss 5ch, 1dc into dc at end of row, turn.

Row 3 1ch, 1ss into each of next 8ch, 1dc through last picot on crescent, *10ch, 1dc into next ch loop*, rep from * to * to end.

Row 4 7ch, 1dc into next ch loop, *6ch, 1dc into next ch loop*, rep from * to * eight times, 6ch, 1dc through next ch loop and first section on pomegranate at same time, **1ss into each of next 6ch on pomegranate, (miss 5ch, 1dc, 5ch on main fabric), 1dc through next ch on pomegranate and main fabric at same time**, rep from ** to ** again. 1ss into each of next 6ch on pomegranate, 6ch (miss 5ch, 1dc, 5ch), 1dc through next ch loop. Make 14ch (miss 11dc), 1dc through dc on pomegranate, 1ss into each of next 11dc back along pomegranate, 1dc into each chain back across to main fabric and back to pomegranate, 1ss into each of next 7dc on pomegranate. Make 20ch (miss 5dc), 1dc back through each of 7dc, *1ss back through each of next 7ch, 13ch (miss 5dc), 1dc through each of next 7dc*, rep from * to * again, 6ch, 1dc into dc. Attach second crescent, 1dc through third picot on crescent, 1ss through each of next 7ch (miss 10dc), 1dc through second picot, 1ss through each of next 7ch (miss 10dc), 1dc through 1st picot, 1ss through each of next 5ch, 1dc through dc at point of crescent, fasten off and finish ends into piece.

JOINING SWIRL AND SECOND POMEGRANATE

Row 1 1dc through ch loop at end of first crescent, *10ch, 1dc through next ch loop*, rep from * to * seven times; **5ch, 1dc into trtr on swirl, 5ch, 1dc into next ch loop**, 4ch, 1dc into trtr on swirl, 4ch, 1dc through ch loop, rep from ** to ** again. Make 10ch, 1dc into next ch loop, 5ch, 1dc through dc at five o'clock point on pomegranate, 5ch,

1dc into ch loop, 4ch (miss 7dc), 1dc through each of next 8dc on pomegranate, 4ch, 1dc through picot on crescent. 7ch (miss 4dc), 1dc through each of next 5dc on pomegranate, 5ch, 1dc through picot on crescent, 8ch (miss 6dc), 1dc through each of next 7dc, 12ch (miss 10dc on crescent), 1dc through picot on cresent, fasten off and finish ends into piece. 1dc through dc at four o'clock on the pomegranate, 4ch (miss 5ch), 1dc through ch loop, 6ch (miss 7ch on swirl), 1dc through trtr, 1ss into each of next 7ch along swirl, 1dc through dc at centre seam on pomegranate, fasten off and finish ends into piece.

FILLING IN THE SHAPE

Part one, Row 1 1dc through ch loop at the top corner of the short end of the serpent, 3ch, miss 1ch, (1tr into next ch, 1ch, miss 1ch) ten times; (1dtr into next ch, 1ch, miss 1ch) ten times; (1trtr into next ch, 1ch, miss 1ch) ten times; (1qdtr into next ch, 1ch, (miss 1ch) seven times; 1ch, miss 6dc on swirl, 1dc into next dc on swirl, turn.

Part one, Row 2 1ch into each of next 7dc along swirl, 2ch, miss 7dc, 1qdtr into next dc, (1ch, miss 1ch, 1qdtr into next qdtr) seven times; (1ch, miss 1ch, 1trtr into next trtr) ten times; (1ch, miss 1ch, 1dtr into next dtr) ten times; (1ch, miss 1ch, 1tr into next tr) 11 times; fasten off and finish ends into piece.

Part two, Row 1 1dc through dc at the opposite end of the serpent, 3ch, miss 1ch, (1tr into next ch, 1ch, miss 1ch) ten times; (1dtr into next ch, 1ch, miss 1ch) ten times; (1trtr into next ch, 1ch, miss 1ch) ten times; (1qdtr into next ch, 1ch, miss 1ch) ten times; 1ch, miss 7dc on swirl, 1dc into next dc on swirl, turn.

Part two, Row 2 1ss into each of next 7dc along swirl, 1ch, miss 7dc, (1ch, miss 1ch, 1qdtr into next qdtr) ten times; (1ch, miss 1ch, 1trtr into next trtr) ten times; (1ch, miss 1ch, 1dtr into next dtr) ten times; (1ch, miss 1ch, 1tr into next tr) 11 times, turn.

Part two, Row 3 1dc through 1st dc, 3ch, miss 1ch, (1tr into next ch, 1ch, miss 1ch) ten times; (1dtr into next ch, 1ch, miss 1ch) ten times; (1trtr into next ch, 1ch, miss 1ch) ten times; (1qdtr into next ch, 1ch, miss 1ch) ten times;

2ch, miss 7dc on swirl, 1dc into next dc on swirl. Fasten off and finish ends into piece.

Part three, Row 1 1dc through picot at the end of first crescent, 1ss into each of next 10ch, *6ch, 1dc into next ch loop*, rep from * to * seven times, turn.

Part three, Row 2 1ss into each of next 7ch around swirl; (1ch, miss 1ch, 1qdtr into next ch) three times; (1ch, miss 1ch, 1trtr into next ch) three times; (1ch, miss 1ch, 1dtr into next ch) three times; (1ch, miss 1ch, 1tr into next ch) three times; (1ch, miss 1ch, 1dc into next ch) three times; (1ch, miss 1ch, 1tr into next tr) three times; (1ch, miss 1ch, 1dtr into next ch) three times, (1ch, miss 1ch, 1trtr into next ch) three times, (make 1ch, miss 1ch, 1qdtr into next ch) to end, 2ch, 1dc into dc below second picot on crescent. Fasten off and finish ends into piece.

EDGING

Right side should be facing you.

Row 1 1dc through dc on corner at short end of the wrap (only one corner remains on the short end; the other corner is now a curve), 6ch, miss 1ch, (1qdtr into next ch, 1ch, miss 1ch) 13 times; (1trtr into next ch, 1ch, miss 1ch) six times; (1dtr into next ch, 1ch, miss 1ch) three times; (1tr into next ch, 1ch, miss 1ch) three times.

Row 2 1dc into each st around entire wrap, fasten off and finish ends into piece.

Beaded bracelet and pendant

Encrusted with a selection of iridescent beads,

the silky rayon yarns of these accessories will

complement a glamorous outfit. Choose beads

in a variety of shades and colours, but keep

them from the same tonal range to ensure that

the pieces will look rich but not fussy.

If you have not crocheted with beads before,

see page 44 for an explanation of the technique.

Materials
50 g (1¾ oz) Sullivans Royal Rayon 3-ply
    crochet yarn (silk yarn may be substituted)
198 assorted small beads (bracelet)
509 assorted small beads (pendant)
1 small button or flat bead, about 1 cm (½ in)
    diameter, for fastening (bracelet)

Tools
1 mm (US 11 or 12/UK 6 or 5½) crochet hook
Sewing needle

Size
Bracelet approximately 21 cm (8¼ in) long, to
    fit small to medium wrist (to adjust for a large
    wrist, use a slightly larger crochet hook)
Pendant 7 x 4 cm (2¾ x 1½ in), excluding
    fringe; chain 100 cm (39 in) long

Tension
30 beaded chain (b/ch) to 10 cm (4 in)

Abbreviations
b/ch: beaded chain
b/dc: beaded double crochet
ch: chain
dc: double crochet

bracelet String beads onto the yarn before commencing the crochet.

finishing the bracelet Sew the button or flat bead onto the end of the bracelet to create the fastening.

Bracelet

WRIST LOOP

String 160 beads onto the yarn. Make 80 b/ch.
Row 1 1ch, *1b/dc in next st, make
3 b/ch, miss 3b/dc*, rep to end, 1dc in last
st. Fasten off and cut yarn, leaving about
(15 cm (6 in) to attach finger loop.

FINGER LOOP

String 38 beads onto the yarn at the end of
the bracelet. Using a sewing needle, fix the
other end of the beaded yarn onto the end
of the bracelet to create a finger loop. Small
beads of similar size such as seed beads are
best for the finger loop, and 38 should make

a loop big enough to fit over a medium-
sized middle finger.

FINISHING

Sew the button or flat bead onto the other
end of the bracelet. The button should
fasten through the loops in the bracelet
chain. Finish ends into work.

Pendant

ORNAMENT

String 112 beads onto the yarn. Make 16ch.
Row 1 Make 1ch, 1b/dc in each st to end,
turn.

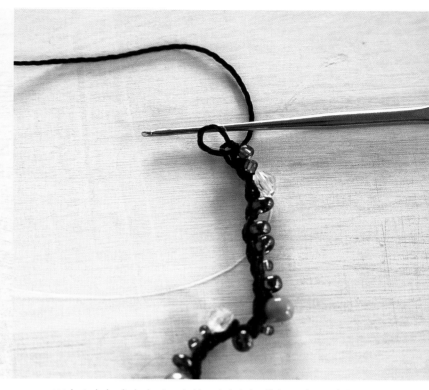

pendant ornament A variety of similarly toned beads are worked into the ornament.

pendant chain A single strand of beaded chain stitch can be made to any length desired.

Row 2 Make 1ch, 1dc in each st to end, turn.
Repeat Rows 1 and 2 another 5 times each.
Next row Repeat Row 1. Finish the ends into work.

FRINGING

String 13 beads onto the yarn and make 13b/ch, to give a short beaded chain. Repeat to make seven chains of varying lengths between 13 and 16b/ch. Using a sewing needle, sew the chains onto the bottom row of the ornament. Finish ends into work.

NECK CHAIN

String 300 beads onto the yarn. Leaving a tail of yarn about 15 cm (6 in) long, make 300b/ch to make a long chain. (The number of beaded chain can be adjusted for a longer or shorter chain; remember to adjust the number of beads also). Fasten off, leaving a tail of yarn about 15 cm (6 in) long. Using the tails of yarn, stitch the ends of the neck chain to the top corners of the pendant.

Hints

To make the bracelet larger or smaller, add or remove beaded chain, allowing four beads per centimetre (½ in).

Any smooth 3-ply yarn can be used for this design. To use a textured yarn, thread the beads onto a nylon filament (invisible thread) and crochet this alongside the main yarn. Lurex can also be crocheted alongside the main yarn to give a different look.

Lampshade

Taking inspiration from the floral prints of Liberty fabrics, this lampshade uses pastel colours and pretty motifs to complement most styles of décor.

Be sure to use materials and yarns in your lampshade that will withstand the heat of the electric globe. Always use flame-retardant spray to treat the yarn, and always use natural fibres for both the yarn and the fabric to cover the lampshade. Man-made fibres may melt from the heat of the lamp.

Materials
50 g (1¾ oz) Debbie Bliss Spun Silk 3-ply yarn in each of Colours 1 and 2
50 g (1¾ oz) TLC Cara Mia 4-ply angora blend yarn (Colour 3)
1 cylindrical lampshade, 33 cm (13 in) long x 46 cm (18 in) circumference
35 cm (14 in) of fabric at least 50 cm (20 in) wide, to cover the lampshade

Tools
3 mm (US 2/UK 11) crochet hook
Low-tack adhesive tape
Adhesive spray
Fabric adhesive
Flame-retardant spray

Size
To fit cylindrical lampshade, 33 cm (13 in) long x 46 cm (18 in) circumference

Tension
Tension is not crucial for this project; the small silk flowers are approximately 2.5 cm (1 in) in diameter and the large silk flowers 3 cm (1¼ in) in diameter

Abbreviations
ch: chain
dc: double crochet
htr: half treble
ss: slip stitch

flower 1 Make 15 flowers in the silk yarn.

loop Create a large loop in chains and double crochet; this will be used to secure the flowers and vines to the inside top edge of the lampshade.

Hints

Different yarns can be used for each of the flowers to give more colour and texture variation.

Variations in yarn thickness will result in different-sized flowers.

FLOWER 1 Make 15

Using 3-ply yarn in Colour 1, make 4ch, join with ss to form a ring.

Round 1 Make 1ch, 9dc into ring, 1ss into ch at beg of rnd.

Round 2 *2ch, 2htr group into next dc, 2ch, 1ss into next dc*, rep from * to * 4 times to make five petals. Fasten off.

FLOWER 2 Make 15

Using 3-ply yarn in Colour 2, make 4ch, join with ss to form a ring.

Round 1 *2ch, 2htr group into ring, 2ch, 1ss into ring*, rep from * to * 4 times to make five petals. Fasten off.

FLOWER 3 Make 15

Using 4-ply yarn in Colour 3, make 4ch, join with ss to form a ring.

Round 1 *2ch, 2htr group into ring, 2ch, 1ss into ring*, rep from * to * 4 times to make five petals. Fasten off.

You should now have a total of 45 flowers. Finish ends into flowers and press carefully.

ASSEMBLING THE LAMPSHADE

Spray the lampshade with adhesive spray, then attach the fabric.

Loop Using 4-ply yarn in Colour 3, make 89ch, join with ss to make a large ring, ensuring that the ring is not twisted.

vines Attach the flowers to crocheted chains through the back of the flowers to make the vines.

flowers Join the vines and flowers to the loop using slip stitch.

Loop, Round 1 Miss 1ch, 1dc in each ch to end, 1ss into 1st ch of rnd.

Loop, Round 2 Miss 1ch, 1ch, 1dc into each dc to end, 1ss into 1st dc of rnd, fasten off. Finish ends into loop.

Vines, Row 1 1ch, 1ss into the centre back of a flower, 1ch, 1ss into the other side of the centre back of the same flower; 10ch, 1ss into the centre back of a second flower, 1ch, 1ss into the other side of the centre back of the same flower; 15ch, 1ss into the centre back of a third flower, 1ch, 1ss into the other side of the centre back of the same flower; 20ch, 1ss into the centre back of a fourth flower; 1ch, 1ss into the other side of the centre back of the same flower.

Attach to the crochet loop using ss, fasten off and finish ends into vine. Repeat 3 times to give four vines, fixed onto the loop 90 degrees apart.

Flowers Tape the loop temporarily to the inside top edge of the lampshade. Incorporate the remaining flowers randomly around the shade, using the same technique as that used to create the vines and varying the number of chains used between each flower, as required. Increase the density of flowers towards the bottom edge of the shade. Fasten off; finish ends into the vines.

Finishing Fix top loop inside top edge of the lampshade using fabric adhesive. Spray entire lampshade with flame-retardant spray.

Hint

Incorporating more flowers will give a more interesting and decorative look; however, adding more flowers will reduce the amount of light that comes through the shade.

Chunky bolster, cushion and throw

Cuddle up on the lounge with cushions and covers in a soft, chunky yarn. It's meant to be comfortable, not chic, so go for faded colours and stippled yarns to bring out the classic cottony texture. This project uses several strands of yarn crocheted together to enhance the chunky, country-style look.

Materials
Bolster: 400 g (14 oz) Jaeger Trinity double-knit silk/cotton blend yarn
  35 x 70 cm (14 x 28 in) soft pillow
Cushion: 250 g (9 oz) Jaeger Trinity double-knit silk/cotton blend yarn
  40 cm (16 in) square cushion insert
Throw: 600 g (1 lb 5 oz) Jaeger Trinity double-knit silk/cotton blend yarn; use a mixture of colours for a patchwork effect

Tools
9 mm (US 13 or 15/UK 00) crochet hook (bolster and cushion)
5 mm (US 7/UK 6) crochet hook (throw)
Darning needle

Size
Bolster: 70 x 35 cm (27½ x 13½ in)
Cushion: 40 cm (16 in) square
Throw: 100 x 85 cm (39½ x 33½ in)

Tension
Bolster and cushion: 11½ sts and 11 rows over patt using 9 mm (US 13 or 15/UK 00) crochet hook and 4 ends of yarn together
Throw: tension is not crucial for this project; 1 motif = approximately 17 cm (6½ in) square, using 5 mm (US 7/UK 6) crochet hook and 2 ends of yarn held together

Abbreviations
ch: chain
dc: double crochet
dtr: double treble
tr: treble

bolster or cushion, row 3 Work a treble stitch into each stitch of the previous row.

bolster or cushion assembly Stitch up the open edges using blanket stitch.

Hints

The bolster and cushion are made using four ends of yarn held together to give a chunky texture. Both covers are made in one piece.

For extra depth of colour, use a contrast-coloured cushion under the cover, as it will show through between the stitches.

For extra interest, try weaving ribbon through the rows of treble stitches (see photograph on page 81).

Bolster

COVER

Make 36ch, turn.

Row 1 1ss into each ch to end, turn.

Row 2 1ch, miss 1 st, 1ss into each ch to end, turn.

Row 3 3ch, miss 1 st, 1 tr into each st to end, turn.

Row 4 1ch, miss 1 st, 1ss into each st to end, turn.

Rows 5 and 6 As for Row 2.

Repeat Rows 3 to 6 until work measures 150 cm (59 in) (approximately 34 repeats), finishing on Row 4. Fasten off and finish ends into piece.

cushion or bolster assembly Allow a 10 cm (4 in) overlap in the middle of one side, through which the cushion or bolster will be inserted.

Substituting yarns

Where possible, you should use the yarn specified in the pattern, as the pattern has been designed specifically for that yarn; other yarns may give different results. However, this is not always possible; the yarn may be discontinued, too expensive or otherwise unavailable. In this case, you will need to find another yarn of similar composition, texture, properties and — most importantly — thickness.

The substitute yarn should crochet to the same tension (see page 23) as the specified yarn, or your finished item will differ in size to the pattern. It is vital to check your tension; even if the specified yarn and the substitute are both labelled as DK, for example, they may differ in thickness.

Be aware that even when the substitute yarn works up to the same tension as the specified yarn, it may give a quite different finished effect. This can be due to various factors, including the yarn's composition and the way it has been treated by the manufacturer. Another reason to do a tension swatch is so you can check you are happy with the look and feel of the fabric that the substitute yarn produces.

ASSEMBLY

Fold widthwise, wrong sides together, allowing 10 cm (4 in) overlap at the centre of one side; the total folded size should be 35 x 70 cm (27½ x 13½ in). Sew up both open edges using blanket stitch. Insert the pillow.

Cushion

COVER

Make 41ch, turn.

Row 1 1ss into each ch to end, turn.

Row 2 1ch, miss 1 st, 1ss into each st to end, turn.

Row 3 3ch, miss 1 st, 1tr into each st to end, turn.

Row 4 1ch, miss 1 st, 1ss into each st to end, turn.

Rows 5 and 6 As for Row 2.

Repeat Rows 3 to 6 until work measures 90 cm (35½ in) (approximately 19 repeats), finishing on Row 4. Fasten off and finish ends into piece.

ASSEMBLY

Fold widthwise, wrong sides together, allowing 10 cm (4 in) overlap at the centre of one side; the total folded size should be 40 cm (16 in) square. Sew up both open edges using blanket stitch. Insert cushion.

throw The throw is worked in different-coloured squares that are then sewn together in an offset fashion, with each at a 90-degree angle to the previous.

square blocks for throw, row 4 The squares are worked in double treble and double crochet.

Throw

SQUARE BLOCKS Make 30

Using two ends of yarn, make 21ch, turn.

Row 1 1dc into each ch to end, turn.

Row 2 1ch, miss 1 st, 1dc into each st to end, turn.

Row 3 As for Row 2.

Row 4 3ch, miss 1 st, 1dtr into each st to end, turn.

Row 5 1ch, miss 1 st, 1dc into each st to end, turn.

Rows 6–7 As for Row 2.

Repeat Rows 4 to 7 another three times. Fasten off. Finish ends into piece. Block each square to shape using a cool iron.

throw assembly Sew the squares together, offsetting each square to the previous at right angles.

variation Weave ribbon through the rows of double treble.

ASSEMBLY

Arrange the squares into a random pattern of colour, offsetting each square by 90 degrees. Using an oversewn seam or blanket stitch, sew together into strips of five squares and then sew the six strips together to create the throw.

If desired, thread lengths of ribbon through some or all of the double-treble rows before sewing up the blocks, to create a contrasting effect.

Hints

The squares are made using three colours of yarn; make squares in two ends of the same colour, or combine two ends each in a different colour to create variegated shades.

For extra depth of colour, back the throw using a complementary coloured fabric, which will show through between the stitches.

Bedlinen trim

Lie in luxury with lovely cotton sheets trimmed with lacy squares of silk yarn. Colour coordinate the crocheted trim with your bedroom décor. The quantity specified will make a trim for a queen-sized sheet and two standard pillowcases. If you want to make a trim for smaller or larger sheets, measure across the top of the sheet and divide by 9 cm (3½ in) — the width of the squares — to determine the number of squares required.

Do make sure that the yarn you choose is colourfast and machine washable, as you will need to wash the sheets and pillowcases with the trim still attached.

Materials:
Four 50 g (1¾ oz) balls Debbie Bliss Spun Silk 3-ply yarn
1 flat queen-size bedsheet, 2 standard pillowcases

Tools
3 mm (US 2/UK 11) crochet hook

Tension
Each motif is approximately 9 cm (3½ in) square

Abbreviations
ch: chain
dc: double crochet
dtr: double treble
htr: half treble
rnd: round
ss: slip stitch
tr: treble

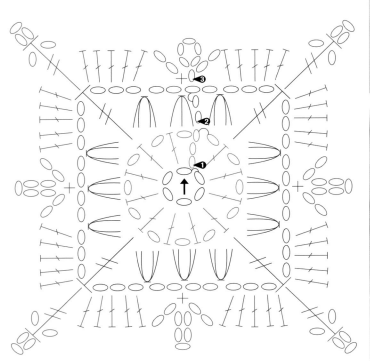

first square motif The second and subsequent motifs are worked in a similar manner, but joined through the picots of the previous motif.

round 2 Work half-treble groups into the spaces of the previous row.

FIRST SQUARE MOTIF

Make 6ch, join with ss to form a ring.

Round 1 4ch, *1tr into ring, 1ch*, rep from * to * 10 times, 1ss into 3rd of 4ch at beg of rnd.

Round 2 2ch, 3htr group in next ch, 2ch, 4htr group in next ch, 3ch, **1dtr in next tr, 3ch, *4htr group in next ch, 2ch*, rep from * to * once, 4htr group in next ch, 3ch**, rep from ** to ** twice, 1dtr in next ch, 3ch, 4htr group in next ch, 2ch, 1ss in top of 2ch at beg of rnd.

Round 3 1ch, *1dc in htr group, 5-ch picot in same dc, 2ch, 5tr into 3-ch loop, 1ch, 1dtr in next dtr, 3-ch picot in dtr just formed, 1ch, 5tr into next 3-ch loop, 2ch*,

round 3 Join subsequent squares at the picots of the previous square.

Be careful not to distort the squares during pressing.

Mercerized cotton is a good alternative to silk: it is less expensive and more resistant to wear.

Always measure sheets before you start work, as many brands differ in size. This pattern is based on a width of 180 cm (71 in) for a queen sheet.

The number of repeats is based on a square which measures 9cm across (picot to picot) when pressed. Use this measurement to work out how many squares to make should you wish to make the trim for a larger or smaller item.

rep from * to * three times, 1ss into dc at beg of rnd. Fasten off; finish ends into piece.

SUBSEQUENT SQUARE MOTIFS

Make 6ch, join with ss to form a ring.
Rounds 1 and 2 As for Rows 1 and 2 of first square motif.
Round 3 1ch, *1dc in htr group, 5-ch picot in same dc, 2ch, 5tr into 3-ch loop, 1ch, 1dtr in next dtr, 3-ch picot in dtr just formed, 1ch, 5tr into next 3-ch loop, 2ch*, rep from * to * once; 1dc in htr group, 5-ch picot in same dc, 2ch, 5tr into 3-ch loop, 1ch, 1dtr in next dtr, 1ch, 1ss through corner picot of first square, 1ch, 1ss in beginning of picot, 1ch, 5tr into 3-ch loop, 2ch, 1dc in central htr group, 2ch, 1ss through centre picot of first square, 2ch, 1ss in beginning of picot, 2ch, 5tr into 3-ch loop, 1ch, 1dtr in next dtr, 1ch, 1ss through corner picot of first square, 1ch, 1ss in beginning of picot, 1ch, 5tr into 3-ch loop, 2ch, 1ss in first htr group. Fasten off.

Repeat subsequent square motif to make a strip of six squares for each pillowcase and a strip of 20 squares for a queen-size sheet. Finish ends into work.

Carefully press the finished strips on the wrong side, then stitch onto the bedlinen.

Filigree drawstring bag

Silky yarn worked in an open design weaves a shining web around a simple taffeta pouch.

Solomon's knot is a stitch for more competent crocheters: it's worth taking the time to practise as it creates such a beautiful lattice of stitches. The length of the stitch is controlled by how long you make the loops; for this project, make them about 3 cm (1¼ in).

Materials
50 g (1¾ oz) ball Debbie Bliss Spun Silk 3-ply yarn
50 cm (20 in) taffeta fabric

Tools
3 mm (US 2/UK 11) crochet hook

Size
Circumference 64 cm (25 in); height 20 cm (8 in)

Tension
The loops of each Solomon's knot should be about 3 cm (1¼ in) long to achieve the size stated above

Abbreviations
ch: chain
dc: double crochet
sk: Solomon's knot
ss: slip stitch

Solomon's knot
Starting with one loop on hook, draw this loop out to desired length. (Using a finger, thumb or thick knitting needle will give a regular sized loop.) Wrap yarn over hook and draw through (as though making an ordinary chain stitch), but with single back thread kept the same length as first long loop, and keeping single back thread of long chain separate from two front threads. Insert hook under this single back thread. Wrap thread over hook again and draw a loop through. Wrap yarn over hook again and draw through both loops on hook. You have now completed one Solomon's knot. Repeat as instructed.

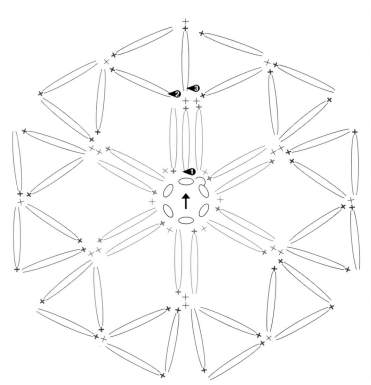

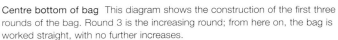

Centre bottom of bag This diagram shows the construction of the first three rounds of the bag. Round 3 is the increasing round; from here on, the bag is worked straight, with no further increases.

round 4 Make a lattice of Solomon's knots.

Hint

To keep track of the rounds, you may find it helpful to put a marker (such as a piece of contrast yarn) at the beginning of each round.

BAG

See page 87 for instructions on working Solomon's knot stitch.

Make 6 ch, join with ss to form a ring.

Round 1 *2sk, 1dc into ring*, rep from * to * five times [six loops], 1sk, 1dc into end of 1st sk at beg of rnd.

Round 2 *2sk, 1dc into centre of next loop*, rep from * to * five times [six loops], 1dc into end of 1st sk at beg of rnd.

Round 3 *2sk, 1dc into end of next sk, rep from * to * to end [12 loops].

Round 4 *2sk, 1dc into centre of next loop*, rep from * to * end [12 loops].

Rounds 5–11 As for Round 4.

Round 12 1sk, 1dc into end of next sk, *5ch, 1dc into centre of next loop*, rep from * to * to end, 1ss into dc at beg of rnd.

Round 13 1ch, 1dc into each st to end, 1ss into 1st ch of rnd.

Round 14 1ch, *1dc into each of next 2dc, 2ch, miss 2 sts, 1 dc into each of next 3dc*, rep from * to * to end, 1ss into 1st ch of rnd.

Round 15 1ch, *1ss into each of next 5ch, 4ch, 1ss into same place as last ss just made (creating picot)*, rep from * to * to end, 1ss into 1st ch at beg of rnd. Cut yarn; finish ends into work.

LINING

1 Cut a 26 x 69 cm (10½ x 27 in) rectangle and a 24 cm (9½ in) circle from the fabric.

round 15 Make picots and holes for the drawstring.

drawstring A twisted cord is threaded through the band for closure.

Overlock or hem the two pieces, and stitch the rectangle into a tube by sewing the ends together along the shorter sides. Turn right side out and stitch along the seam again, concealing the raw edges inside a French seam; see Hint, at right. (The wrong side of the fabric now becomes the outside of the tube.)

2 Pin the circle to the end of the tube (wrong sides together), and stitch. Turn the bag inside out and restitch the bottom seam as a French seam.

3 Fold the top edge over twice and stitch flat. Pleat the top of the lining bag so it measures the same width as the crochet bag. Turn the lining with the right side on the outside and put it inside the crochet bag. Pin the two bags together and stitch around the top edge.

DRAWSTRING

Cut two lengths of yarn each 2 m (2 yards) long and knot together at either end. Secure one end and twist the other end until the yarns are tightly twisted (about 100 twists). Fold them in half and allow them to twist up on themselves, making a rope. Use a crochet hook to feed the rope in and out of the eyelets in the band around the top of the bag. Tie a knot near the top of the remaining rope and another towards the end. Trim off the ends.

French seams

To make a French seam, join the fabric with wrong sides together, stitching close to the edge (about 6 mm/¼ in seam allowance). Carefully trim the fabric close to the stitching line, then press the seam flat. Now fold the fabric along the stitching line so that the right sides are together, and press. Stitch the seam along the seam allowance (about 6 mm/¼ in from the edge). The raw edges of the fabric will be concealed inside the seam allowance.

Openwork stole

This lacy stole, with its motifs of snowflakes and swirls, is designed to wrap around the shoulders, with both cuffs being worn on the same arm for a snug fit.

The yarn — a hand-dyed blend of silk, mohair and wool — will be surprisingly cosy despite the open pattern of the crochet work.

Materials
150 g (5½ oz) Noro Silk Garden

Tools
5 mm (US 7/UK 6) crochet hook

Size
Appproximate widths: Size S, 130 cm (52 in) from cuff to cuff; Size M 150 cm (59 in); Size L 170 cm (66 in)

Tension
Snowflake motif = 22 cm (8½ in) diameter after pressing
Swirl motif = 20 cm (8 in) diameter after pressing

Abbreviations
ch: chain
dc: double crochet
dtr: double treble
qdtr: quadruple treble
ss: slip stitch
tr: treble

snowflake, round 3 Work groups of three treble stitches into the points.

snowflake, round 4 Work picots on the points of the outer row.

SNOWFLAKE Make 5 (6, 7)

Make 9ch, join with ss to form a ring.

Round 1 8ch, *3tr into ring, 5ch*, rep from * to * another four times, 2tr into ring, 1ss into 3rd of 8ch at beg of rnd.

Round 2 1ss into next ch, 7ch, 4tr into 1st 4-ch loop, *1ch, 4tr into next 4-ch loop, 4ch, 4tr into same 4-ch loop*, rep from * to * another four times, 1ch, 3tr into 1st ch loop of rnd, 1ch into 3rd ch at beg of rnd.

Round 3 1ss into next ch, 6ch, 3tr into first ch loop, *3ch, 3tr into 4-ch loop, 3ch, 3tr into 4-ch loop*, rep from * to * another four times, 3ch, 2tr into ch loop at beg of rnd, 1ch into next ch of ch loop.

Round 4 1ss into each of next 2ch, 8ch, 1ss into 4th ch just made (making a 4-ch picot), 1ch, 2tr into 1st ch loop, *5ch, 1dc into 3-ch loop, 5ch, 2tr into next 3-ch loop, 5ch, 1ss into 1st ch just made, 1ch, 2tr into same 3-ch loop*, rep from * to * another four times, 5ch, 1dc into 3-ch loop, 5ch, 1tr into ch loop at beg of rnd, 1ss into 3rd ch at beg of rnd. Fasten off. Finish ends into piece.

SWIRL Make 4 (5, 6)

Make 9ch, join with ss to form a ring.

Round 1 3ch, *1tr into ring, 2ch*, rep from * to * another six times, 1tr into 1st ch loop at beg of rnd.

Round 2 4ch, 1dtr into next ch space, *4ch, 1dtr into next tr, 4ch, 1dtr into next

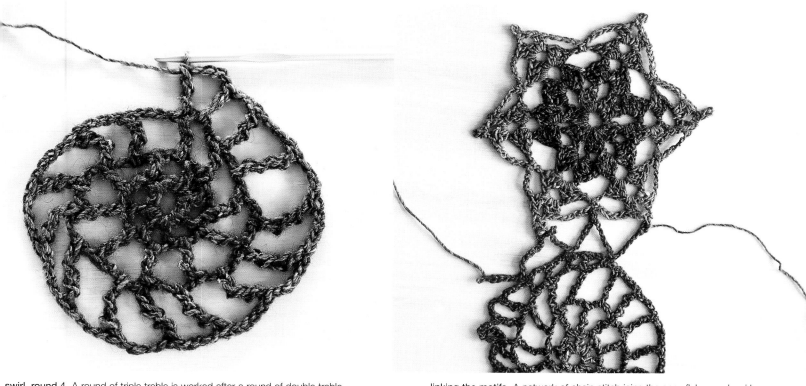

swirl, round 4 A round of triple treble is worked after a round of double treble.

linking the motifs A network of chain stitch joins the snowflakes and swirls; see Diagram 1, on page 94.

ch space, 4ch, 1dtr into next ch space, 4ch, 1dtr into next ch space*, rep from * to * again.

Round 3 4ch, 1trtr into next ch space, 4ch, 1trtr into next dtr, 4ch, 1trtr into next ch space, 4ch, 1trtr into next dtr, *4ch, 1trtr into next ch space, 4ch, 1trtr into next ch space, 4ch, 1trtr into next dtr*, rep from * to * twice.

Round 4 *4ch, 1dtr into next ch space, 4ch, 1dtr into next dtr*, rep from * to * another three times, 4ch, 1tr into next ch space, 3ch, 1tr into next trtr, 3ch, 1tr into next ch space, 2ch, 1tr into next trtr, 2ch, 1dc into next ch space, 1ch into next ch. Fasten off. Finish ends into the piece.

LINKING THE MOTIFS
Press all of the snowflakes and swirls, without distorting their shape (see Hint).

Row 1 Make 1ch through 1st picot on first snowflake, 5ch, 1dc through dc at beginning of first swirl, 8ch, (miss 1ch, 2tr, 5ch), 1dc through dc on snowflake. Make 6ch, (miss 2ch, 1tr, 2ch), 1dc through tr on swirl. Make 8ch (miss 5ch, 2tr, 1ch), 1dc through picot on snowflake. Make 7dc, (miss 3ch, 1tr, 3ch), 1dc through tr on swirl.

Row 2 7ch, 1dc through picot on second snowflake, 5ch, (miss 4ch, 1dtr, 4ch), 1dc through dtr on 1st swirl, 8ch, (miss 1ch, 2tr, 5ch), 1dc into dc on snowflake, make 8ch, (miss 4ch), 1dc through dtr on swirl, make

Hint

Use a warm iron and pressing cloth to press the motifs. The pressing cloth will prevent the motion of the iron from pulling and distorting the shapes.

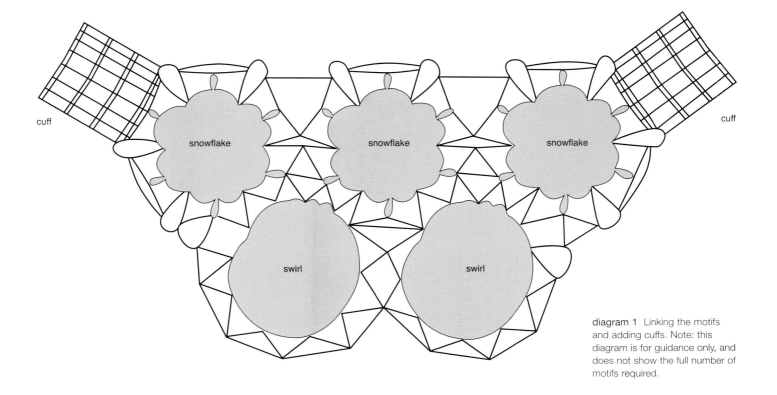

diagram 1 Linking the motifs and adding cuffs. Note: this diagram is for guidance only, and does not show the full number of motifs required.

Hint

The correct way to wear the stole is with the snowflakes at the top. Both cuffs should be pushed up on one arm with the stole draped over the opposite shoulder. However, it you intend always to wear it in the conventional way, as a draped wrap, omit the cuffs.

8ch, (miss 5ch, 2tr, 1ch), 1dc through picot on snowflake.

Repeat Rows 1 and 2 until all snowflakes and swirls have been incorporated. Fasten off and finish ends into piece.

Row 3 1dc through picot adjacent to picot on first snowflake, *make 14ch, (miss 1ch, 2tr, 5ch), 1 dc through dc, make 14ch, (miss 5ch, 2tr, 1ch), 1dc through picot*. Repeat from * to * another three times. **Make 8ch, 1dc through picot on next snowflake, 7ch, 1dc though 14-ch loop on previous snowflake, 7ch, (miss 1ch, 2tr, 5ch), 1dc through dc on second snowflake. Make 7ch, 1dc through next 14-ch loop on first snowflake, make 7ch (miss 5ch, 2tr, 1ch),

1dc through next picot on second snowflake, *make 14ch, (miss 1ch, 2tr, 5ch), 1dc through dc, make 14ch (miss 5ch, 2tr, 1ch), 1dc through picot*, rep from * to * twice.** Repeat from ** to ** until you reach the end of the snowflakes. Make 14ch, (miss 1dc, 8ch, 4ch, 1dtr, 4ch), 1dc into dtr at the end of fourth swirl. *Make 14ch, (miss 4ch, 1dtr, 4ch), 1dc through dtr*, rep from * to * around fourth swirl. **Make 8ch, 1dc through dc on previous swirl, make 7ch, 1dc though 14-ch loop on previous swirl, make 7ch, (miss 4ch, 1trtr, 4ch), 1dc through trtr on second swirl. Make 7ch, 1dc through next 14-ch loop on first swirl, make 7ch, (miss 4ch, 1trtr, 4ch), 1dc through next trtr on

cuffs Work in rows of quadruple treble alternating with double crochet.

cuffs Wear both cuffs on the same arm, or omit the cuffs to give a draped wrap that can be worn in the conventional way.

second swirl, *make 14ch (miss 4ch, 1trtr, 4ch), 1 dc through trtr*, rep from * to * another four times.** Repeat from ** to ** twice (until you reach the end of the swirls). Make 14ch, 1dc into 1st picot on first snowflake, make 14ch, (miss 1ch, 2tr, 5ch), 1dc into dc, make 14ch (miss 5ch, 2tr, 1ch), 1dc into picot, fasten off and finish the ends into the piece.

Row 4 Make 1dc through first loop on first snowflake, *make 8ch, 1dc through next loop*, rep from * to * the entire way round the stole, fasten off and finish the ends into the piece.

CUFFS

Row 1 Join yarn through point at far end of the stole, 1dc into each of the next 16ch, turn.

Row 2 Make 6ch, *1qdtr into next st, 1ch, miss 1dc*, rep from * to * to end, 1qdtr into last st.

Row 3 Make 1ch, *1dc into each st to end. Repeat Rows 2 and 3 twice, fasten off and finish ends into the piece. Stitch the end of the cuff onto the back of the snowflake to create the cuff loop.

Repeat at other end to create another cuff.

Bath mat and mitt

The bathroom is the one room of the house where luxury is a necessity. With a mat to keep your wet feet off the cold floor, and a soft scrubbing mitt to buff your skin to a healthy shine, you'll never want to leave.

Cotton yarn is absorbent, washable, and soft to the touch, so it's perfect for use on bare skin. Cotton also becomes softer the more it is washed, so the more you use it, the nicer it becomes.

The pictured examples use five different shades to give graduated stripes.

Materials
Jo Sharp Soho Summer double-knit cotton yarn:
  300 g (10½ oz) for Mat; 100 g (3½ oz) for Mitt

Tools
Mat: 5 mm (US 7/UK 6) crochet hook
Mitt: 4 mm (US 5/UK 8)crochet hook

Size
Mat: 48 x 35 cm (19 x 14 in)
Mitt: 18 x 13 cm (7 x 5 in)

Tension
Mat: 13½ sts and 8 rows = 10 cm (4 in) in bouclé
  loop crochet using 5 mm crochet hook and 2
  ends of yarn held together
Mitt: 20 sts and 13 rows over 10 cm (4 in) in
  double crochet using 4 mm crochet hook and
  one end of yarn

Abbreviations
ch: chain
dc: double crochet
blc: bouclé loop crochet (see below)

Bouclé loop crochet
Bouclé loop stitch is worked on a base of double
  crochet (US single crochet). The following
  instructions are for right-handed crocheters: Hold
  yarn with left hand and, with right hand, wrap
  yarn clockwise around left index finger to make a
  loop. Insert the hook into the stitch so there are
  two loops on the hook. Pass the hook *over* the
  yarn (not under, as usual). Catch both strands of
  yarn with the hook, and pull them both through
  the stitch. You should now have 3 loops on the
  hook. Wrap the yarn over the hook and draw the
  yarn through all loops on the hook. You have
  now completed one bouclé loop stitch. Repeat
  as required.

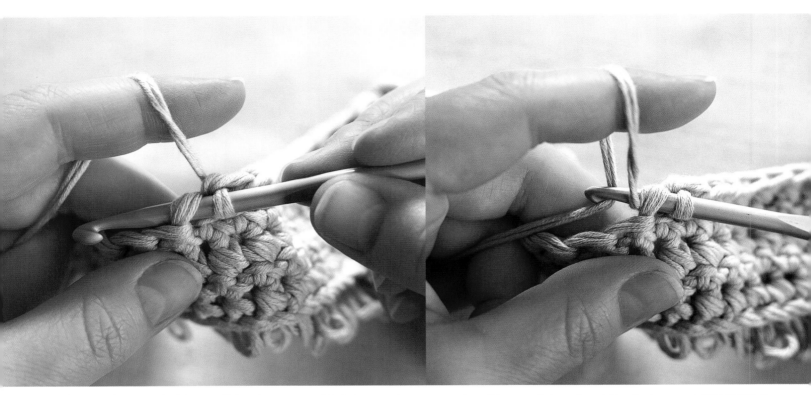

bouclé loop crochet Insert hook in next stitch and wrap yarn anticlockwise around index finger of left hand.

bouclé loop crochet, continued Pass hook over yarn (not under it, as is usual) and draw both strands through to front of work.

Mat hint

To achieve a graduated stripe effect in the mat, simply use two strands of yarn together, each of a different colour, and change the colour combination every couple of rows. The sequence for this piece is: shade 1 + 1, shades 1 + 2, shades 2 + 2, shades 2 + 3, shades 3 + 3, shades 3 + 4, shades 4 + 4, shades 4 + 5, shades 5 + 5, shades 5 + 4, shades 4 + 4, shades 4 + 3, shades 3 + 3, shades 3 + 2, shades 2 + 2, shades 2 + 1, shade 1 + 1 (working from dark to light and back to dark).

Bath mat

Using two ends of yarn, make 45ch, turn.
Row 1 1blc into each ch to end, turn.
Row 2 1ch, miss 1blc, 1dc into each st to end, turn.
Row 3 1ch, miss 1dc, 1blc into each st to end, turn.
Repeat Rows 2 and 3 another 33 times, changing colours every 4 rows in the order suggested in the Hints, at left, or at random. Fasten off; finish ends into piece.

bouclé loop crochet, continued Pass yarn under hook again and draw through
I loops on hook. Hold the loop with your finger until the stitch is complete

Bath mitt

PLAIN SIDE

Make 31ch, turn.

Row 1 1ss into each ch to end, turn.

Row 2 1ch, miss 1 st, 1ss into each st to end, turn.

Rows 3–17 As for Row 2.

Row 18 1ch, 1ss into each of first 3sts, 1dc into each of next 24sts, 1ss into each of last 3sts, turn.

Row 19 As for Row 18.

Rows 20–23 As for Row 2.

Row 24 1ch, 1ss into each of first 3sts, 1dc into each of next 24sts, 1ss into each of the last 3sts, turn.

Row 25 As for Row 2.

Repeat Row 18 six times; rep Rows 24 and 25; rep from * to * again.

Repeat Rows 18 and 19.

Row 42 1ch, 1ss into each of first 2 sts, 1ss into next 2 sts together (to decrease), 1dc into each of the next 23 sts, 1ss into each of last 3 sts, turn.

Row 43 1ch, 1ss into each of first 2 sts, 1ss into next 2 sts together (to decrease), 1dc into each of the next 22 sts, 1ss into each of the last 3 sts, turn.

Continue in this manner, decreasing 1 st at beginning of each row, until 18 sts remain. Fasten off and finish ends into piece.

Mitt hint

Like the mat, the mitt is worked in stripes, with the colours changing every couple of rows. Work from dark to light and back to dark for a graduated effect, or mix the colours up at random.

mitt Use five graduating shades of colour for a subtle stripe effect.

plain side The mitt has one plain side and one bouclé loop side.

BOUCLÉ LOOP SIDE

Make 31ch, turn.

Row 1 1ss into each ch to end.

Row 2 1ch, miss 1 st, 1ss into each st to end.

Repeat Row 2 another 15 times.

Row 18 (WS) 1ch, miss 1 st, 1ss into each of next 3 sts, 1blc into each st until 3 sts rem, 1ss into each of final 3 sts, turn.

Row 19 1ch, 1ss into first 3 sts, 1dc into each of the next 24 sts, 1ss into final 3 sts, turn.

Row 20 As for Row 18.

Repeat Rows 19 and 20 another seven times.

Repeat Row 19 again.

Row 36 1ch, 1ss into each of the first 2ch, 1ss into next 2 sts together (to decrease), 1blc into each of the next 23 sts, 1ss into each of the last 3 sts, turn.

bouclé loop side, odd rows Work double crochet every second row.

finishing Crochet the two sides of the mitt together around the edges, with wrong sides together.

Row 37 1ch, 1ss into first 2 sts, 1ch into next 2 sts together (to decrease), 1dc into each of the next 22 sts, 1ss into each of the last 3 sts, turn.
Continue in this manner, decreasing 1 st at the beginning of each row, until 18 sts remain.
Fasten off and finish ends into work.

FINISHING

Hold the two mitt pieces with the right sides out (the loopy side of one and the slightly more textured side of the other), crochet together around the edges, using ss.
Fasten off and finish ends into the piece.

Tea cosy

Just the way grandma used to make it, a steaming pot of tea is a one of life's everyday pleasures. Keep your tea hot with this crocheted cosy, which is simply constructed from squares.

These square motifs could be adapted to make other accessories, from placemats to throws and even scarves.

Materials
50 g (1¾ oz) TLC Cara Mia 4-ply angora blend yarn
1 button, approx 15 mm (⅝ in) diameter

Tools
4 mm (US 5/UK 8) crochet hook

Size
To fit most 4-cup teapots

Tension
1 motif = 10 cm (4 in) diameter after pressing

Abbreviations
ch: chain
dc: double crochet
dtr: double treble
htr: half treble
ss: slip stitch
tr: treble

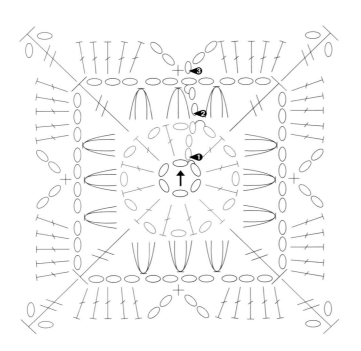

first square motif Work subsequent squares slightly differently.

row 3 At the corners, work 1dtr into the corner dtr of the previous row.

FIRST SQUARE

Make 6ch, join with ss to form a ring.

Round 1 4ch, *1tr into ring, 1ch*, rep from * to * 10 times, 1ss into 3rd ch at beg of rnd.

Round 2 2ch, 3htr group in next ch, 2ch, 4htr group in next ch, 3ch, **1dtr in next tr, 3ch, *4htr group in next ch, 2ch*, rep from * to * once, 4htr group in next ch, 3ch**, rep from ** to ** twice, 1dtr in next ch, 3ch, 4htr group in next ch, 2ch, 1ss in top of 2ch at beg of rnd.

Round 3 1ch, *1dc in htr group, 2ch, 5tr into 3-ch loop, 1ch, 1dtr in next dtr, make 1ch, 5tr into 3-ch loop, 2ch*, rep from * to * another three times, 1ch in 1st dc at beg of rnd. Fasten off and finish ends into piece.

SECOND AND THIRD SQUARES

Make 6ch, join with ss to form a ring.

Rounds 1 and 2 As for the first square.

Round 3 1ch, *1dc in htr group, 2ch, 5tr into 3-ch loop, 1ch, 1dtr in next dtr, 1ch, 5tr into 3-ch loop, 2ch*, rep from * to * once; 1dc in htr group, 2ch, 5tr into 3-ch loop, 1ch, 1dtr in next dtr, 1ss through corner ch of first square, 1ch, 5tr into 3-ch loop, 2ch, 1dc into 1htr group and through centre edge of first square at same time, 1ch, 5tr into 3-ch loop, 1ch, 1dtr in next tr, 1ss through corner of first square, 1ch, 5tr into 3-ch loop, 2ch, 1ss in 1st dc of rnd.

Repeat to create and attach a third square.

row 3 Join subsequent squares as you crochet row 3 of the pattern

FOURTH SQUARE

Make 6ch, join with ss to form a ring.

Rounds 1 and 2 As for the first square.

Round 3 1ch, *1dc in htr group, 2ch, 5tr into 3-ch loop, 1ch, 1dtr in next dtr, 1ss through corner of first square, 1ch, 5tr into 3-ch loop, 2ch, 1dc in next htr group, 6ch, 1ss in dc just made (makes button loop), 2ch, 5tr into 3-ch loop, 1ch, 1dtr in next dtr, 1ss through corner of first square, 1ch, 5tr into 3-ch loop, 2ch, 1dc in next htr group, 2ch, 5tr into 3-ch loop, 1ch, 1dtr in next dtr, 1ss through corner of 3rd square, 1ch, 5tr into 3-ch loop, 2ch, 1dc in htr group and through dc in third square at same time, 2ch, 5tr into 3-ch loop, 1ch, 1dtr in next dtr, 1ss through corner of third square, 1ch, 5tr into 3-ch loop, 2ch, 1ch in dc at beg of rnd. Fasten off and finish ends into work.

FINISHING

Attach button to edge of first square, in line with button loop on fourth square.

Hints

The teapot spout fits into the upper or lower split between the second and third squares. The handle fits into the split between the first and fourth squares. The button secures through the handle. The cosy fits most four-cup pots.

For an alternative finish, use textured yarn, or a yarn with a high wool content and felt up, using liquid soap and warm water. (Use thicker wool and a larger hook to allow for shrinkage in the felting process.)

Fingerprint oven gloves

Protect your hands from hot dishes and pans with this cute pair of oven mitts. Crochet them in colours to match your kitchen décor – we've used a variegated denim-look cotton thread. They are decorated with a pretty whorl of stitches, just like a giant fingerprint.

Cotton is a good choice of yarn for items that will be exposed to hot temperatures: man-made yarns may melt, while woollen yarns may felt up and lose the lovely texture of the stitches.

Materials
100 g (3½ oz) Rowan All Seasons Cotton yarn
25 cm (10 in) cotton fabric
25 cm (10 in) cotton batting

Tools
4 mm (US 5/UK 8) crochet hook
Darning needle

Size
20 x 15 cm (8 x 6 in)

Tension
16 sts and 10 rows in pattern = 10 cm
(4 in)

Abbreviations
ch: chain
dc: double crochet
htr: half treble
ss: slip stitch
tr: treble

fingerprint Work in a continuous spiral of stitches of varying size.

glove in progress Make four pieces.

Hint

No two fingerprints are identical, so why not make one 'fingerprint' a little different from the other by slightly varying the rounds of stitches.

FINGERPRINT Make 2

1 Make 4ch, join with ss to form a ring. Work in a continuous spiral around the ring.
2 Make 1ch, 8dc into ring, 2dc into each of 1st 2dc. *From here on, work into back loop only of each st:* 2tr into each of next 6dc, 2tr into each of next 19 sts, *2tr into next tr, 1tr into next tr*, rep from * to * another 14 times, **1tr into each of next 2tr, 2tr into next tr**, rep from ** to ** another 20 times, 1htr into next tr, 1dc into next tr, 1dc into next tr, 1ss into next tr. Fasten off and finish ends into piece.
3 Repeat steps 1 and 2 to make a second circular fingerprint.

GLOVE Make 2

Make 25ch, turn.
Row 1 1ch, 1dc into each ch to end, turn.
Row 2 3ch, 1tr into each dc to end, turn.
Row 3 1ch, 1dc into each tr to end, turn.
Repeat Rows 2–3 another four times.
Row 12 1ch, 1dc into 1st dc, 1htr into next 2dc together (to decrease), 1dc into each dc to end. Repeat Row 12, decreasing each time until the final row is 10dc in length. Fasten off and finish ends into piece.
Repeat three more times to make four glove pieces.

Attaching fingerprint Darn a fingerprint motif onto one side of each glove.

lining and batting Stitch around the sandwich of fabric and batting.

FINISHING

1 Take two glove pieces and place with right sides together. Darn together around the side and top edges using blanket stitch. Turn right side out.

2 Take one fingerprint and darn onto the outside of the glove.

3 Repeat Steps 1 and 2 to assemble the second glove.

4 Measure six 1 m (1 yard) lengths of yarn and tie them together with a knot at one end. Plait the yarn into a three-strand plait. This is the cord to keep the gloves together.

5 Using one of the gloves as a template, cut four glove shapes from the cotton batting and four glove shapes from the cotton fabric (cut the cotton fabric slightly bigger than the batting). Overlock or hem the cotton fabric to stop it from fraying.

6 Place two pieces of the cotton fabric with the right sides together, then place a piece of cotton batting on either side. Stitch the sandwich of fabric around the side and top edges, but not at the wrist opening.

7 Insert this glove, still with right sides together, inside the crocheted glove, place one end of the cord into the inside corner of the wrist edge, and stitch around the wrist edge to hold everything in place.

8 Repeat steps 6 and 7 a second time to complete the second glove.

Hints

The circular 'fingerprint' piece makes a good pot stand on its own: simply increase or decrease the number of rounds for the appropriate size.

It is not advisable to use alternative fibres for this piece. Cotton withstands heat extremely well (better than most other natural fibres), while synthetic fibres will melt at relatively low temperatures. Cotton also wears well and washes easily.

Index

Published in 2007 by Murdoch Books Pty Limited
www.murdochbooks.com.au

Murdoch Books Australia
Pier 8/9, 23 Hickson Road, Millers Point NSW 2000
Phone: +61 (0) 2 8220 2000   Fax: +61 (0) 2 8220 2558

Murdoch Books UK Limited
Erico House, 6th Floor North, 93–99 Upper Richmond Road, Putney, London SW15 2TG
Phone: +44 (0) 20 8785 5995   Fax: +44 (0) 20 8785 5985

Chief Executive: Juliet Rogers
Publisher: Kay Scarlett

Concept: Tracy Loughlin
Art direction: Vivien Valk
Designer: Jacqueline Richards
Project manager: Janine Flew
Editor: Melody Lord
Project designer and maker: Stephanie J. Milne
Photographer: Natasha Milne
Stylist: Sarah O'Brien
Production: Adele Troeger

National Library of Australia Cataloguing-in-Publication Data

Milne, Stephanie J. Crochet : designs. Includes index.
ISBN 9781740458917. ISBN 1 74045 891 5.
1. Crocheting - Patterns. I. Title. (Series : Handmade style). 746.434041

Printed by 1010 Printing International Limited in 2007. PRINTED IN CHINA.